HOLOCAUST MEMORIAL CENTER
28123 Orchard Lake Road
Farmington Hills, MI 48334-3738

Grandpa's Mountain

Letters from a border Kibbutz in Israel

Arieh Larkey

ARTZY BOOKS
JERUSALEM ◆ NEW YORK

Other books by Arieh Larkey:

A Townhouse in Jerusalem
Ruth – Revisited: A Survivor's Journey
Landscape of Conflict: Israel's Northern Frontier

Grandpa's Mountain: Letters From a Border Kibbutz in Israel
Published by ARTZY Books
Text Copyright © 2007/5767 by Arieh Larkey

TYPESETTING: Jerusalem Typesetting
COVER DESIGN: Benjie Herskowitz with Arieh Larkey

Hard Cover ISBN: 978-1-932687-87-3

E-mail: publisher@devorapublishing.com
Web Site: www.devorapublishing.com

Printed in Israel

To the dreamers and "boy scouts"
of all ages – everywhere.

Part 1

December 20, 1996

Mr. Yoram Friedman
c/o Kibbutz Misgav-Am
Israel

Dear Grandpa Yoram,

I hope this letter gets to you. I found your address on an old letter you sent to my Dad a long time ago. I think I was maybe three years old then. Now I'm twelve years old. I asked my Dad about you but he says he doesn't want to talk about you. I don't understand why. Did you have a fight with my Dad?

I am writing to you because I don't think my parents understand me. I heard them talking about you one time and they called you a dreamer and a Boy Scout. Are you still in the Scouts? I just joined Troop 48 at our temple. I want to become an Eagle Scout. Are you an Eagle Scout? One of the requirements is a 14-mile hike and my parents won't let me go because it's wintertime and it's too cold. I'm no sissy! Maybe you could write to them and ask them to let me go. Thank you.

Your grandson and fellow Boy Scout,
Steven Friedman.

P.S. What's a kibbutz?
P.P.S. Maybe someday I can come to visit you.

January 10, 1997

Master Steven Friedman
1053 Claremont Road
Livingston, New Jersey 07039
U.S.A.

Dear Steven,

What a pleasant surprise it was to receive your letter. I'm not sure whether my response will reach you, either. I hope so!

As to your first question – yes, I was in the Scouts during my teenage years and I made Eagle when I was fifteen. Even though I lived in the city (Newark) the Boy Scouts gave me an opportunity to discover the beauty and mystery of the great outdoors. *My* parents weren't exactly thrilled, either, when I went on overnight hikes in the middle of winter, but I won them over slowly with my enthusiasm and growing knowledge of outdoor survival techniques. Maybe patience and time will work for you, too.

My parents' main concern was that I keep my grades up, despite my new, time-consuming hobby. I must admit to you now, this was a bit difficult at times, since I seemed to be always daydreaming about my next camping trip. Due to my lack of interest in school-work, I was forbidden to go on camping trips until I brought my grades up. My parents were right, of course, and I thank them to this day for helping me to realize that a good basic education is a solid foundation for the future.

Regarding the answer to the question in your first P.S. – What is a kibbutz? – I'll try to explain. A kibbutz is a special type of farming community, which is owned and run by the people who live there – all the adults, that is. The children go to school just like you and also join the Scouts and other Israeli youth organizations. Your father was in one of them, as I recall.

On our farm, we grow many different things. We have apple,

2

peach and pear orchards up in the hills on our kibbutz, and we also grow wheat and cotton in the valley below. But the most interesting of all our projects, at least for me, is our fresh-water ponds (like small lakes) which we built ourselves in order to breed fish for sale to our local markets. I worked in the fishponds for many years. I'm sort of retired now, but I help out in our kindergarten during the morning. We have twelve children and they're all very sweet. They like it best when I tell them stories.

I don't think it would help if I wrote your parents about the 14-mile hike, but keep trying. Even if they still say no, springtime isn't far off.

I would love to hear from you again, so if you have a chance, please write.

With love,
Grandpa

P.S. Your handwriting is really nice!

February 7, 1997

Dear Grandpa,

I got your letter. I think Mom and Dad read it first, because the envelope was already open, but that's okay. It was really nice to receive your letter. What you wrote me about loving the outdoors is how I feel, too. Mom and Dad don't understand. I would really like to talk to you about it without my parents reading the letters. Do you have e-mail? We could chat every day about camping and being in the woods and maybe canoe trips. Did you ever go on a canoe trip? The older boys in our Scout troop were telling us about a 5-day canoe trip they took last summer down the Delaware River. I hope I can go on a trip like that this summer.

Your kibbutz sounds very interesting. I'd like to live on a farm.

You said your kibbutz is up in the hills. Could you send me a picture? Why did you move to Israel? Maybe you could tell me more in your next letter or e-mail. My e-mail address is stevief@aol.com.

    Your grandson,
      Steven Friedman.

                                      April 5, 1997

Dear Steven,

    Sorry to have taken so long to respond to your last letter. I don't have e-mail, so I guess we'll have to stick with these "old-fashioned" letters. I'm sure your parents will respect our privacy.

    I'm happy to tell you more about kibbutz life, and I'm glad you find it interesting. Our kibbutz is thinking about making some changes to the basic laws (rules and regulations) of how we run our little community and I've been quite busy with these issues. As I mentioned in my last letter, all the adults who live here (about a hundred of us) are owners, and therefore each of us has a say in how we run our affairs. We have meetings where we discuss everything and then we take a vote, just like the U.S. Congress does when they want to make changes to the laws or to make new laws. If you would like to know more, please let me know.

    In your last letter, you asked why I moved to Israel. I guess I could give you some simple explanation about Zionism (the Jewish resettlement of the biblical Land of Israel) but it would be much more interesting for both of us if I travel back in time to the days when I was just about your age. The person I am today, and the decisions I made along the way, all began back then.

    The year was 1948 and I was about to be bar mitzvah'ed. I could finally say goodbye to Hebrew school, which I attended in the afternoons (after regular school) for the previous four years. Boy, was I really looking forward to that! More freedom and more time for my newfound love of the great outdoors. I had joined the Boy Scouts the year before, and I was well on my way to becoming an Eagle Scout. I was already a Star Scout; I had seven merit badges – with just three more to go for Life, and then on to Eagle. Just like you, my whole life revolved around my love of the outdoors: hiking, camping and canoe trips down the very same river your friends talked about – the Delaware. Yes, 1948 was a very special year for me. According to the rituals of the Jewish faith, I "became a man." Not quite, but according to my memories, I felt I was well on the way.

But something else – something much more important – also happened that year. I heard my parents talking about it, but I really didn't pay that much attention. Someplace – halfway around the world – the newly created Jewish State of Israel was fighting a war of independence. What did that have to do with me? I was an American Boy Scout and on my way to achieving its highest award – Eagle Scout.

To be continued!... More about hiking and camping in my next letter.

Please say hello to your parents for me.

> With love,
> Grandpa

April 29, 1997

Dear Grandpa,

I got your letter a couple of weeks ago. I didn't write back right away because, last Sunday, I finally got to go on that 14-mile hike. I waited so I could write you all about it. I was really excited to hear that you were an Eagle Scout and that you went on canoe trips like the one I want to do. Please tell me more about it in your next letter.

Now I want to tell you all about our hike. I think all the parents, not just mine, wanted our scoutmaster to wait until it got warmer. It was pretty cold back in January so the hike was postponed. We all met at the JCC at 8 in the morning. Mom packed my knapsack with 3 sandwiches and 2 of her special brownies. Do you know what brownies are? Mom's are the best! We also had to bring a canteen of water.

Our scoutmaster, Mr. Grossman, led us on the hike from the JCC in Livingston to the scout campgrounds in the South Orange Mountains. There were about 10 of us on the hike, which is one of the requirements to become a First Class Scout. When we got there, we had lunch and then practiced First Aid and how to start a fire with flint and steel and also by spinning a wood stick, like a bow and arrow, into a piece of wood until smoke comes out. I tried but I didn't make a fire. I'll keep practicing!

Mr. Grossman said it was about 7 miles each way. The hike back was a little harder than in the morning. We stopped a lot to rest, but we finally got home about 6 o'clock. I really slept good that night. This summer our troop is going to summer camp for 2 weeks. I'm really excited about that.

Please write back soon.

Your grandson,

Steven

P.S. I forgot to tell you that I like to swim. We have a pool at the Jewish Community Center here in Livingston.

P.P.S. I hope to take the Junior Life Guard course this summer at camp.

June 5, 1997

Dear Steven,

I've been a bit busy with kibbutz business lately, but I haven't forgotten my new pen pal in the States. Your last letter reminded me so much of my own scouting days. I remember that 14-mile hike as if it were just yesterday – but, in fact, it was exactly fifty years ago this month. And from the way you described the scout campgrounds in the South Orange Reservation, I think we hiked to the very same place in the spring of '47. Since we all lived in Newark, we met at Irvington Center and hiked from there to South Orange.

It sounds like things haven't changed all that much in half a century – at least in the Boy Scouts. I also went to camp that summer – Camp Mohican, up in northern New Jersey (Sussex County). It was somewhere near the town of Blairstown. Maybe you can find it on a map. That summer, my kinship with nature really took root. It's true that we all liked the Scouts – camping and hiking was really fun for all my friends – but I seemed to take to the outdoors more naturally than the other boys. Considering that I was a city kid, I felt very much at home and comfortable in my new surroundings – the forest.

I remember one time that first summer, when my friends and I wandered off into the woods by ourselves. They turned back – fearing the unknown. I continued on, alone, deep into the woods, where the shadows of my imaginary monsters frolicked with the chipmunks and squirrels, and tiny creepy-crawly creatures made their way from rock to crevice to forest floor in an endless procession that kept my attention for hours. Suddenly, without warning, darkness fell and I could no longer see my newfound friends. I was alone in the forest at night, but for some reason, I was not afraid – I felt I was not *really* alone. Somehow, God made his presence known to me out there in the middle of my private playground. He has been my constant companion ever since.

I eventually made my way back to camp, only to be met by a very angry camp director, who threatened to send me home if I ever wandered off again. Apparently a search party had been sent out to look for me when I hadn't returned to camp by nightfall. I promised that I wouldn't wander off again and all was forgiven.

But after that experience, my life was never quite the same. I had discovered a special part of myself that needed to be nourished with increasing regularity. I craved camping and hiking as though they were an essential part of my young life – just like school, only my extra-curricular classroom was the great outdoors and my teacher was non other than Mother Nature herself.

And that's how my lifelong love affair with the great outdoors began – that summer of '47 at Camp Mohican. Instead of just the two-week session, I convinced my parents to let me stay for the whole summer. That's how I got to go on my first *real* adventure – hiking on the Appalachian Trail. I'm enclosing an old photograph for you. That's me, with the big pack on my back.

More to come in my next letter.

Love,

Grandpa

June 26, 1997

Dear Grandpa,

After I got your letter, I asked my scoutmaster if he'd ever heard of Camp Mohican. He said that he had, but that it isn't there any more. The Scout camp moved to another place a long time ago. That's where we're going in August. It's called Camp Leni-Lenopee. I looked on a map of New Jersey and I found Blairstown. I think our camp is also near there. We also might go on an overnight in July. I hope so! My scoutmaster said he hiked on the Appalachian Trail, too. I looked it up on the Internet and wow! It goes all the way from Maine to Georgia. Did you hike all that way? Please tell me all about it. I have to say goodnight now because I'm very tired from playing basketball.

Your grandson,
Steven

P.S. I can't sign off without thanking you for the picture you sent me. Your knapsack looks really heavy!
P.P.S. How old were you then? Is that the Appalachian Trail?

July 13, 1997

Dear Steven,

Your last letter brought back such wonderful memories for me that I want to share them with you. The name of the new Boy Scout camp – Leni-Lenopee – was especially nostalgic, since at the age of fifteen, I was inducted into the "Indian" tribe of Leni-Lenopee in a secret ceremony that I will never forget... Now, before you start thinking that your grandpa is starting to tell "tall tales" about his boyhood days, let me explain.

First of all, the Leni-Lenopee were a real tribe of American Indians (Native Americans) who lived peacefully in the Delaware and

Leheigh Valleys for hundreds of years before the white man came along and, over time, confiscated their land. The native population simply disappeared into the lost pages of American history. They had once been a proud tribe of the larger Mohican Nation, which occupied the lands of the present-day northeastern United States, all the way from the Canadian border in upper New York State, down through the Delaware and Leheigh Valleys of New Jersey and Eastern Pennsylvania.

If you're interested, look up their history on the Internet, or, better yet, find a copy of the novel *The Last of the Mohicans* by James Fenimore Cooper. I'm sure your local library has a copy. Even though it's a fictional account, it does give you a feeling for a part of Native American folklore at a time in American history when the white man was becoming dominant on the North American continent, which he believed at the time to be his "Manifest Destiny." I know that's a pretty fancy term, but it is the single, most important concept that shaped the United States of America as you know it today. Again, if you're interested, look it up. It puts American history into a perspective that is often overlooked and that has been overshadowed by the momentous events that have taken place in this chaotic twentieth century.

Anyway, getting back to my original story or more accurately put – a legend – which originated in the latter part of the last century – a young Indian boy from the Leni-Lenopee tribe and a white boy who lived in a settlement close to his village both happened to have wandered into the forest one day – alone. The white boy was a new settler and, not knowing the dangers that awaited him in this unfamiliar environment, was suddenly struck in the leg by the fangs of a diamondback rattler. It had warned of its impending attack by the distinctive sound of its rattles – but to no avail. The boy was unfamiliar with the warning and, after several minutes of sheer panic, he lay helpless on the ground as the poison began to spread throughout his body.

Hearing the faint moaning of the stricken boy carried along by the soft winds that swept through the forest at sundown, the Indian boy began to search out the sounds, which eventually led him to the boy's side. Carrying the almost unconscious victim on his back, the Indian youth headed back towards his village several miles away. They arrived just as darkness descended.

A runner was sent to the white settlement to bring the boy's already-distraught parents, who immediately followed him back to the village where the tribal medicine man and his strange poultice (bandage or compress) had begun to work their "magic" on the boy's swollen leg and soaring high fever. Miraculously, by the next morning, the fever had broken and the boy opened his eyes to the grateful smiles of his parents and, off to one side of the teepee, the vaguely familiar face of the boy who had carried him from the woods – saving his life.

During the next few months, the two boys became fast friends. Through the innocence of their youthful friendship, they were able to bypass the inherent mistrust and prejudice of their parents' generation. They became more than just friends. They became "blood brothers," symbolically mingling their blood through small cuts on the palms of their hands. According to legend, it was this extraordinary act of friendship during a time of mutual distrust, even hatred, between their two peoples, that spawned the concepts of brotherhood and fellowship between the white man and his Native American counterpart.

Although these lofty principles never really took hold in mainstream, turn-of-the-century American society, they were adopted by a new youth movement that was just beginning to spread across the United States with the dawn of the new century – the Boy Scouts of America. To keep the bond with the past and its Native American origins, a secret "Indian" society was created within the scouting movement itself. It became known as the *Order of the Arrow* – a symbolic rebirth of the Leni-Lenopee tribe. Only a few outstanding campers were selected each summer to join this special band of Scouts whose ideology would be based – for life – on the principles of brotherhood and fellowship. I was inducted into the "Order of the Arrow" during my third summer at Camp Mohican – at the age of fifteen.

That's all for now. Have a wonderful time at camp. I'm looking forward to hearing all about it when you return home.

Love,

Grandpa

July 29, 1997

Dear Grandpa

I got your letter a few days ago. I've been busy packing for camp, which starts on Sunday. I'm really excited. We're leaving from the JCC. Our troop is taking a special bus, which leaves at 9 AM and gets to camp around noon. I'll take your letter with me so I can read it again. I'm also taking my dictionary because there were some words I really didn't know, but that's okay, I like to learn new words. Your letter was really interesting even if I didn't understand everything. I'm sure when I read it again, I'll have lots of questions to ask. I'll try and send you some postcards from camp too.

Your grandson,

Steven

September 10, 1997

Dear Grandpa,

I had a super summer. I want to tell you all about it. First, I took your letter with me and I read it over and over again. It's such a beautiful story and I have to tell you something. It's all true. Just like you wrote me about. I feel I can only talk with you about it because we're the same. I think I want to start over and tell you all about summer camp and everything that happened.

We got to camp around 12 o'clock and our troop was assigned to Indian Point Village, which is right on the lake. We lived in 4-man tents. In our tent was me, Joel Glick, Barry Feldman and Marvin Pollack (the senior patrol leader). We were right next to the lake, which I really liked because I could hear the water splash onto the rocks. In the morning I got up real early so I could look at the lake before the sun came up. It looked like steam was coming up from the water.

After breakfast, which we all ate in a big dining hall, there were different activities. I was signed up for the Junior Life Guard Course, so I spent all morning at the waterfront. I passed the course, so now I can wear the Red Cross badge on my bathing suit. (Mom already sewed it on for me.) After lunch, there were other activities you could choose. I went to Woodsmanship, where we learned camping skills, like how to build different kinds of shelters in the woods, and how to lash logs together with rope. We built a lookout tower and an Indian teepee that way. We also learned which wild plants you can eat and which ones you can't, and how to build a fire from those wood sticks I wrote you about once. This time I did it! I actually made a fire the way cavemen probably did.

Our counselor's name was Ted Pappendorf, but we called him Pappi. He knows everything about the outdoors. I learned so much from him. When I found out that he was going to lead a hike on the Appalachian Trail during the last 2-week session of camp, I begged Mom and Dad to let me stay on past my session. They finally said yes. When our first two weeks was finished, I was the only one from our troop to stay over. At the last flag-lowering ceremony (before the others left), something special happened. All of a sudden, some older boys came out of the woods dressed up as Indians. Each one of them wore a white sash with a red arrow on it. The leader told us that at the end of each session they choose a few of the best campers to join a special scouting club called the *Order of the Arrow*. Grandpa, it was just like you wrote me about in your letter. They called it a "tapping-out" ceremony because they walk slowly from troop to troop, and then suddenly stop in front of a boy and tap him on the shoulder 3 times and then he follows them back into the woods. Out of the whole camp they only picked 7 boys. Our senior patrol leader, Marvin Pollack, was one of them. All through the ceremony I was thinking about what you wrote in your last letter. I can't stop thinking about it. Maybe someday they'll pick me.

Grandpa, I have to stop now because I have a lesson for my bar mitzvah, which will be in November. Do you think you can come? I really hope so!

Your grandson,
Steven

P.S. Did you get my postcards from camp?
P.P.S. Mom and Dad are getting me a Hewlett-Packard color printer for my bar mitzvah. I've already picked it out. Now I can type my letters to you on my computer.

September 20, 1997

Dear Steven,

First, I want to wish you and your mom and dad a very happy and healthy Rosh Hashana (שנה טובה). We here in Israel pray each year, and in fact each day, for peace with our Palestinian neighbors. Peace has eluded us for so long. Maybe this year it will come!

Steven, thank you so much for inviting me to your bar mitzvah. There isn't anything in this world that I'd rather do than be with you and the family for this very special event in your life. But sometimes, we're just not able to do the things we most want to do. To my great sadness, this is one of those occasions. I must tell you honestly that I believe my coming would make your dad and grandma very uncomfortable because of the differences we've had in the past. I hope, with all my heart, that someday soon your dad, grandma and I will be able to overcome those differences and forgive each other, but unfortunately, that day is still to come.

I will be there with you in spirit when you're chanting your *haftora* at temple. I'm sure you're going to make your parents and grandma very, very proud. And me too! You are my son's son, and that is a very special bond between us that will only grow stronger with time. God willing, I will be with you for many more milestones in your life. Your bar mitzvah is only the first of many to come. Let's think about the future, okay? Mazal tov, Steven; my love will always be with you.

It seems that the camping bug has skipped a generation. You seem to be just as enthusiastic about the great outdoors as I was at your age. In that regard I want to send you a special bar mitzvah present, but I have to ask your parents' permission. I'll send them a separate note about it. In order not to keep you in suspense, I'll forgo the element of surprise and tell you now what it will be.

A good camping knife is one of the essential tools that a serious camper keeps with him at all times. I want to send you the best. It's handmade by the Randall Company of Orlando, Florida. Randall-made knives are famous all over the world. As a matter of fact, the first astronauts in the Mercury Program of the 1960s took specially made Randall knives into space. In Vietnam and the Gulf War, Randall fighting knives saw combat with the U.S. Special Forces and the Marines. I've had my Randall camping knife for over fifty years now, and it remains at my side, even today, whenever I venture out into the woods. It's a small version of the famous "Bowie Knife," named after Colonel Jim Bowie who fought at the Alamo with Davy Crockett and the other brave patriots of early American history.

The story of Jim Bowie and his legendary fighting knife was made into a 1950s movie called "The Iron Mistress," starring Alan Ladd, if I remember correctly. Bowie was quite a hero in his day. If you'd like to find out more about him, I'm sure it's on the Internet. A replica of his original knife is on permanent display in the

Smithsonian Institute in Washington DC. As a matter of fact, I am the proud owner of an identical replica of that famous fighting knife, which is mounted in a glass case on the wall of my study. I'm enclosing a picture of it. Actually, there's quite a story of how I came to have such a prized collector's item. It brings back some wonderful memories for me, which I thought I might share with you now.

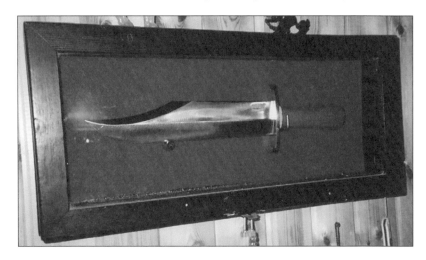

All the way back in my own early Boy Scout days – at age twelve or thirteen – I was just glancing through the Boy Scout magazine *Outdoor Life* when I spotted an advertisement for Randall camping knives. I immediately sent away for their free catalogue. A few weeks later it came… and I was hooked! I had to have their camping knife (the one I'm sending you) but it was expensive. On my $5 weekly allowance it would take me a while to save up. Babysitting on the weekends contributed to my "camping knife fund." When I was fifteen, I was finally able to send away for it and it's been with me ever since – like a trusty friend.

But that's not the story of the big Bowie you see in the picture. That first catalogue also showed a picture (and the astronomical price tag) of the replica of Jim Bowie's fighting knife. It was love at first sight. Someday, I promised myself, I was going to have that knife. It was just a young boy's dream, but it lasted through the decades as I grew into adulthood. Periodically, I'd send away to Randall for their latest catalogue and, sure enough, it was still there – in full color – and still very expensive. It was just my private little dream but, in the course of time, I shared it with your grandma after we met and got married. But it was still just my fanciful dream. I'm sure you have your unrealistic dreams too. We all do. Well, I'm here to tell you that sometimes, as fanciful as they may be, those private dreams do come true!

For my thirty-eighth birthday – right here in Israel – your grandma actually ordered my "dream" from the Randall Company in Orlando, Florida. Isn't that incredible? She sent away for it many months in advance in order to be sure it got here in time. But how to keep it a secret from me – that was her challenge. If it was sent through the regular mail or a special delivery service, I would surely have found out, since you had to sign for all packages from outside the country. And then there was the customs duty to be paid. What could she do? Somehow, through family friends in the States, she located someone who was coming to Israel on a visit and who agreed to bring it in her luggage. In today's world that just wouldn't be possible. The knife would certainly be found and confiscated – and the person would probably be detained for questioning!

And so, after I blew out the candles on my birthday cake, your grandma brought out this mysterious package. I will never forget that birthday! I was in total shock. The knife was even engraved with my name! Now, how's that for a "dream-come-true" story?

Before I sign off, I want to congratulate you on passing your Junior Lifeguard course. I'm sure your swimming and lifesaving skills will give you many years of pleasure. I still splash around in our kibbutz pool on a pretty regular schedule – three or four times a week. Swimming is probably the best overall sport to keep in shape – especially for us *seniors*!

I loved hearing about your first summer at camp and look forward to hearing the next installment, about your first hike on the Appalachian Trail

Well, that's about all for now. Looking forward to your next letter.

Love,

Grandpa

P.S. I received all your postcards. Your camp looks really beautiful. I'm sorry that I didn't save any of the photographs from Camp Mohican, which I could have shared with you now. I would never have imagined back then, that – fifty years into the future – I would have an opportunity to share my own youthful adventures with (of all people) – my grandson. Life sure holds some wonderful surprises in store for us!

September 21, 1997

Dear Grandpa,

I just finished my algebra homework, and now I can finish telling you about this past summer. It was the best summer of my life. After my troop left, Pappi let me bunk with him and another counselor, in their tent, because they had an extra bed. I really felt special because they treated me like one of them. The other counselor's name was Tom, and he was on the waterfront staff. He saw me swimming in the Junior Lifeguard course, and he told me that I had a really good stroke and to keep at it. He said that maybe I could even work on the waterfront next summer as a junior staff member. That made me feel really good but I think I'd rather go hiking on the Appalachian Trail again, or maybe go on that canoe trip down the Delaware River.

Now I want to tell you everything about my first hike on the Appalachian Trail.

I was really surprised to find out that Pappi was just taking five of us on the hike. We met at our tent on Monday morning after breakfast. At first I felt weird, because all the boys were older and bigger than me. They had come up to camp just to go on this hike with Pappi. The oldest guy, Carl, was 17, and going into his senior year in high school. I'm still in junior high! Jerry and Arthur were both 15, and Franklin was 14. I was only 12½. I'll be 13 in November. In one way, I felt a little strange to be the youngest, but it also made me feel really good to be doing the same things they'd be doing, even though I was younger and smaller than them.

They all brought their own personal hiking equipment, like fancy backpacks, lightweight sleeping bags and hiking boots and everything. All I had was my Nikes, but Pappi said they would be okay for this first hike. For next summer, though, I should get a sturdy comfortable pair of hiking boots, like Timberlands. Pappi lent me a lightweight sleeping bag, made with duck feathers, and it was really warm. He also lent me a really comfortable backpack. I had most of the other stuff.

We practiced packing our backpacks so they were balanced, and we went over all the important things to take, like waterproof matches and toilet paper and stuff. We all shared carrying the food. Some of it was dried and in plastic bags, like mountain climbers take, and some of it was fresh. Everyone (except me) already had a walking stick made from a strong branch with its bark peeled off and a sort of a v notch at the bottom, so it can be used as a snake stick (to pin down the snake's head). There are rattlesnakes and copperheads in this part of the country, so we had to be prepared. I hate snakes, but I didn't want to tell Pappi because he loves catching them and putting them in this snake pit we have at camp. They call him The Snakeman. Anyway, I spent 2 or 3 hours out in the woods, looking for just the right branch to make into a walking stick for myself. I found one, and shaved off the bark (just like the others). It felt really good in my hand, and Pappi said it was perfect. It helps you keep your balance with a big pack on your back, and when you're climbing over rocks and stuff. (But I'm sure you know all about that, Grandpa.) Pappi showed us on a map just where we were going to hike. We would be on the trail for 5 days, hiking about 60 miles (there and back).

Grandpa, I'm tired now. To be continued… I'm back. It's Sunday morning now. I got up early so I could finish this letter, because I'm meeting my friends at the park at 10 o'clock to play basketball. Now, back to the Appalachian Trail!

We started out real early in the morning, because Pappi wanted to reach our first night's campsite by around 4 in the afternoon. We took a small trail from right in back of the dining hall, which led up into the hills above the camp. After about an hour of hiking up the mountain, we finally reached another trail. Pappi showed us a sign attached to a tree. It's the symbol that shows when you're on the Appalachian Trail ⚹. I was really excited to be hiking on the same trail you hiked on when you were a boy. I even told Pappi and the other boys about you. They were really interested, and wanted to know about Israel and your kibbutz (none of them are Jewish).

My pack was heavy but my new walking stick helped me keep my balance. Pappi was in the lead, and even though he's short he hiked pretty fast. I was right behind him and I tried really hard to keep up, which I did. We stopped to rest at lookout points on the trail, where the views were really great. We could see for miles. We also met some people hiking the trail in the opposite direction and talked to them for a while. We stopped for lunch at a really special lookout point. I never knew New Jersey was so beautiful. I guess that's why they call it the "Garden State."

We were on the trail for 5 days and 4 nights, making the round trip from our camp to the Delaware Water Gap and back. Three states come together up there (New Jersey, New York, and Pennsylvania). After hiking about 15 or 16 miles the first day, with that heavy pack on my back, I really slept great that night. I was a little sore when I got up in the morning, but by lunchtime I was fine. I think the thing I remember most about the hike is the scenery and how big New Jersey is, even though it looks so small on a map (compared to other states). I'll always remember how much fun it was sitting around the campfire at night and telling stories. This time I just listened, but maybe next time, I'll be able to tell a story or two myself.

Grandpa, it's about time for me to meet my friends now. Please write soon. I really enjoy your letters.

Your grandson and fellow hiker,
    Steven

October 1, 1997

Grandpa, Wow!

I just got your letter with the photo enclosed. What a fantastic knife! It looks even bigger than the knife in the Rambo movies. Do you ever use it, or do you keep it on the wall, like a picture?

That was a great story you wrote me about Grandma's birthday present to you. Does she know that you still have the knife? I'm sure she would be happy. Can I show her the picture the next time we go over to visit her?

Grandpa, I'm really excited about the camping knife you're going to send me. Mom and Dad got the letter you sent them, and they said it's okay. I looked up Jim Bowie on the Internet and I downloaded 3 pages about his life. He was really famous. I'm also going to try and get the video of that movie about his life. The Blockbuster at the mall probably has it. They have a whole section on old classics.

Grandpa, I'm really sorry you can't come to my bar mitzvah. I'll write you all about it. My bar mitzvah teacher made a tape of my *haftora* and I've been listening to it on my Walkman while I do my homework. I already know it by heart.

School is okay, but I can't wait till next year when I can try out for the swimming team. I want to race free-style and butterfly. Do you know what the butterfly stroke is? Our high school took the State Championship last year. Some of my friends and I went to cheer for our team. It was so exciting I came home hoarse from cheering so hard.

Grandpa, I can't wait till the knife comes but I'm also sorry you can't come to my bar mitzvah.

Love,
Your grandson,
Steven

November 15, 1997

Dear Grandpa,

The knife just came by UPS Delivery Service all the way from Orlando, Florida. It's fantastic!!! It looks just like the picture you sent me of the real Bowie knife, only smaller. It's got a leather sheath with a pocket for a small sharpening stone. Grandpa, it's the best present I ever got. I can't wait to take it on my next camping trip. I'm going to bring it to our scout troop meeting this Thursday night. I've been telling my friends about it since your last letter. Now they can really see it. I also showed them the picture you sent me of the big Bowie. Besides being a beautiful knife, it's a part of American history as well.

Your present came just in time for my bar mitzvah next Saturday. I'm not really nervous because I know everything by heart. But I'm really sorry you can't come. Mom and Dad are making this big party at a place called the Chanteclair in Milburn. It's a real fancy place, and they invited a lot of people. I got to invite 10 of my friends from school and the Scouts. I'll write you all about it.

Grandpa, you haven't written in a while. Are you okay? Thank you very much for the knife. I love you.

Your grandson and fellow camper,
Steven

December 8, 1997

Dear Steven,

I enjoyed reading your description of your hike on the Appalachian Trail. It brought back a lot of wonderful memories for me. I'm so delighted that you like the Bowie camping knife. Use it well and enjoy many more camping trips in the future with it at your side.

Sorry I haven't written in a while. I'm fine! I've just been very busy lately. Our kibbutz has just decided to build a small private housing community on our land for rent to non-members. This is a giant break from our past tradition and not all the members agreed with the idea. However, a majority vote gave it the go-ahead and, before I knew what had happened, I was elected to head up the project. At first I was reluctant to take it on, but when I thought it over, I realized that it would be a great challenge for me – which is very important, at my age.

I'll be hiring surveyors, as well as the architect and engineers and, most difficult of all, I'll be working with the local municipality to get all the building licenses approved. It's a bit complicated to explain, but since the government wants to create incentives for young couples to move up north, especially in order to develop our growing hi-tech industry here in Kiryat Shmona (our closest town), they are full partners with us in financing this project. It will be a good future source of income for the kibbutz, even though we will have to share our little Garden of Eden with outsiders who weren't a part of its creation.

We're going to be building twenty new houses on the slopes of our mountain, which looks out onto an incredible view. I'm sure by now that you've pinpointed us on a map of Israel and have noticed that we are situated directly on the border with Lebanon. I'll try to describe our unique location for you.

To the north and west lies the rugged high country of southern

Lebanon. To the east, the gently rolling hills of the Hula Valley below, once a vast mosquito-infested swampland, now cradles many sister kibbutzim in its drained fertile acreage. At the eastern edge of the valley, a high plateau known as the Golan Heights makes its way from the south, rising dramatically – directly opposite our kibbutz – into a magnificent peak called Mount Hermon, over 2,000 meters above sea level. I'm enclosing a photograph (taken from our porch), looking across the valley towards our snow-capped mountain. It's pretty spectacular, isn't it? I discovered this little "Shangri-La" over thirty years ago, together with my wife and son (your grandma and your dad). Your dad was only ten years old back then. It's a long story, but the gist of it is that, after several years, your grandma and your dad decided that life would be better for all of us back in America. I thought otherwise, and decided to stay. I couldn't leave. I had found my home. This tiny corner of our planet somehow gave me inner peace, even though the political situation here in Israel was far from peaceful.

And so our little family broke apart. Your grandma and dad

returned to the States, restarting the lives they had left four years earlier. I'm sure it wasn't easy. And I remained here in Israel – on my kibbutz – carving out a life that I felt had meaning for me.

I don't think it would be a good idea to ask your dad or grandma about it, because it's a very sensitive and painful part of our family history. I promise I'll explain everything as we continue our correspondence, but what's most important for you to know now is that the break-up of your grandma and me, as well as the bad feelings that exist between your dad and myself, are nobody's fault. Things happened back then, events that we had no control over. And those events, and our individual reactions to them, determined the decisions we each made about our futures.

Let's get back to your bar mitzvah. How was it? I'd love to hear all about it and about school too. It's wintertime now, so I'm not sure if you're going on overnights, but I'd love to hear about your everyday adventures in Livingston, NJ. When I was a young boy growing up in Newark, I'm not sure if the township of Livingston was even built yet. That's it for now.

With love,
Grandpa

P.S. Happy Hanukkah to all.

December 19, 1997

Dear Grandpa,

What a fantastic picture of your view of Mount Hermon! I really like how you write. I don't always know all the words, but I look them up in my Webster's Dictionary. I showed the picture to Mom and Dad and Dad said he remembers it very well. He didn't say anything else and I didn't ask, just like you told me.

Happy Hanukkah, Grandpa. We light the candles every night and sing a song called "Maoz Tzur." Do you know that song? Our temple has a big electric menorah in the front garden. Tonight's the fifth night.

My bar mitzvah at temple was really nice. I guess I did my *haftora* very well, because Rabbi Hirsh shook my hand a lot after I finished. Mom and Dad were really proud of me too. The party at the Chanteclair was really nice, except I had to shake hands with all my relatives (Mom's got a lot on her side) and all my parents' friends. I didn't have much time to spend with my own friends that I invited. The food was really good, though! I'm sorry you weren't there.

We haven't gone on any camping trips yet this year, but our scoutmaster is trying to get all the parents to let us go on a winter overnight, even if there's snow on the ground. He told us about cutting branches from evergreen trees to use as a cushion over the snow before we pitch our tent. Then we put down a waterproof tarpaulin, and then our sleeping bags on top of the tarp. It sounds like it should keep us warm and dry. I hope we get to go. I brought my camping knife to our Scout meeting and everyone really liked it. Our scoutmaster, Mr. Grossman, liked it so much that he's going to order one just like it from that company in Florida.

Things in school are okay. Next year I'm going into the ninth grade, which is the first year of high school. Seventh and eighth grades are junior high, even though we're in the same school. Next year I can try out for the swimming team. In junior high we have all sorts of clubs after school, but not varsity sports. I just joined the Junior Debate Club. I thought it would be kinda interesting, because in history we're studying the Civil War, and in debate club we're going to be debating States' Rights versus the Federal Government, and that's what started the war between the North and the South, like who has the right to decide about slavery in the state and stuff. President Lincoln was assassinated after that war.

My Dad told me not to ask you any questions about politics in

Israel, but I have to ask you just one. Why was your President Rabin assassinated? I don't know why President Kennedy was either.

Please write soon.

Love, your grandson,
Steven

January 8, 1998

Dear Steven,

It sounds like your bar mitzvah went smoothly and I'm very proud of you too. Mazal tov! At my own bar mitzvah, I didn't understand any of the Hebrew I recited by rote. Strangely though, when I moved to Israel where Hebrew is the language of the land (not just in prayer books) all those strange Hebrew characters I learned as a bar mitzvah boy would begin to make sense. I could never have imagined, back then, that this archaic language of the Bible would come back into my life in future years. And that it would be the language I would speak on the street... and buy my groceries with. That would have been simply inconceivable for me to believe as a young tennage boy growing up in America. And yet, a few decades later, it would be so!

Anyway, let's get back to this decade and some (cold) current events. Last week I saw a news report on CNN about that really big blizzard that hit the whole upper east coast of the United States. I'll bet it was fun for you and your friends. I heard the schools closed for two or three days.

When I was your age, and a really big snowstorm hit, my friends and I loved it. We earned a lot of money shoveling snow from our neighbors' driveways. We also liked to go sledding. We all had sleds called "Flexible Flyers" because you could sort of steer them with the front handles – a little bit. Anyway, back in Newark, I lived on a street called Hedden Terrace. In back of our house was a big undeveloped plot of land, with lots of hills that were just perfect for sledding. We even gave the hills special names, according to the degree of danger or the number of bumps or twists and turns. The most dangerous, and the most fun of course, was called "Suicide Hill." Nobody ever *really* got hurt, but we did take some pretty scary spills, now and then.

Your question about the assassination of Yitzhak Rabin has been on my mind since I received your last letter. It's not easy to answer, but I'll try. First of all, I want to take a moment to explain the differences between Israel's *President* and our *Prime Minister* – we have both. Yitzhak Rabin was our Prime Minister, who is the elected head of our government. Our President is appointed, and it is a "ceremonial" position. The president hosts the foreign diplomats and dignitaries who come to our country, but he doesn't deal with the everyday politics and policies of our government. Our present Prime Minister is Mr. Ehud Barak of the Labor Party, and our President is Mr. Ezer Weizmann. We have a lot of political parties, even religious parties (unlike the U.S., which is supposed to have a strict separation of "church and state"). The two main parties are Labor and Likud – sort of like the Democrats and the Republicans in the United States.

Prime Minister Rabin was the leader of the Labor Party. He was assassinated on the evening of November 5, 1995, after attending a peace rally in Tel Aviv. I shall never forget that night as long as I live. I cried all night long, and simply stared at the television news during the next surreal day, as he was brought to his final resting-place on Mount Herzl, in Jerusalem.

I'm sure you're aware of our struggle for peace here in Israel. Sometimes it seems that we get more news coverage on international TV networks than even the United States. Israel is a small country (about the size of New Jersey) that is inhabited by two peoples – we Jews and the Palestinians. Somehow we have to find a way in which both peoples can live in peace and prosperity on this small strip of land, on the eastern coast of the Mediterranean Sea.

The "Oslo Peace Accords", signed in Washington in 1993 by Prime

Minister Rabin and the Palestinian leader, Chairman Arafat, and witnessed by President Clinton, envisioned a two-state solution to the problem; the State of Israel living side by side with a newly-created Palestinian State, carved out of a portion of this land which we both inhabit. I know that sounds very complicated – and it is!

It will take very difficult and painful compromises on both sides in order for this dream of peace to become a reality. There are people (both Jews and Palestinians) who oppose *any* sort of compromise. The man who shot down our prime minister is just such a man – a Jewish fanatic who could not envision any compromise that would bring about peace between the Jews and the Arabs who inhabit this ancient and holy land. He will remain in jail for the rest of his life.

The "peace process" is still alive, and we are continuing our dialogue with the Palestinians to try to bring an end to our long and difficult struggle. Maybe peace will come to our land this year. Our daily prayers are for a just and lasting peace with all our Arab neighbors, including Syria, Lebanon and the rest of the Arab world.

I hope I've answered your question. I probably went overboard in my explanation, but as you can imagine, it's pretty complicated and emotional. For the time being, at least, let's talk about less serious subjects like camping and hiking, school, my kibbutz and things like that – okay?

Love,
Grandpa

January 20, 1998

Dear Grandpa,

Thank you for telling me about Prime Minister Rabin. I remember watching TV with Mom and Dad about his funeral. Even President Clinton was there.

I really liked hearing about your winters in Newark. These days in our neighborhood, most everyone has a snow-clearing machine, like a small tractor, so I can't earn money like you did, but we do go sledding. It's not as exciting or as dangerous as in your day, but it's fun. Some of my friends like to iceskate on the frozen lake in our park, and one of my friends even skis with his dad in the mountains in New York State.

Winter is okay, but I like summer better, because I can go camping and hiking a lot. I can't wait! I called Pappi to find out what the plan is for next summer at camp. He lives in Nutley, NJ. He's a schoolteacher. He teaches wood shop in a vocational high school. Anyway, he said that this summer he's going to lead a 5-day canoe trip down the Delaware River. I'm really excited!

Grandpa, I want to talk to you about something I can't talk about with Mom and Dad. I feel sort of funny, but you're my pen pal, so I thought maybe I could ask you. There's this girl in my class that I really like. Her name is Barbara Williams. I would like to maybe ask her out to the movies or something, but I don't know how to bring it up. My friends and I talk about girls and stuff, but none of us has gone on an real date with a girl. She sits right next to me in algebra, and we talk about the answers to equations and things like that, but that's all. I don't know how to ask her out to the movies or maybe even just to walk around the mall together. I'm sort of bashful about talking to her that way. She's really nice and she's pretty too.

I wish you lived closer, so I could really talk to you. Why did you move to Israel? Do you think you could come to visit me sometime?

Grandpa, I have to finish my homework so I'll sign off.

Love,
Your grandson,
Steven

P.S. Barbara isn't Jewish.

February 8, 1998

Dear Steven,

Sorry for taking so long to respond to your last letter. I've been really busy with my work. I'll explain about that later, but first let me try to respond to your questions.

I'll answer your last question first, because I think it's by far the most challenging – how to get along with girls. Steven, my answer is probably not what you anticipated or wanted, but I hope it will suffice for the time being. There's a natural progression to life. What comes to mind is how a baby learns to walk. The baby attempts to stand and it falls back down. But, unshaken by that first unsuccessful attempt, it tries again. This time it succeeds. Within the blink of an eye, the baby is not only standing, but is taking its first steps. True, they are unsure, but they are real steps and will become more sure as time passes. This is what life is all about. Give it a go, Steven. Just do it! Ask her out… and good luck!

As to your other question – Why did I move to Israel? – I think for now, I'd like to answer it with an old Native American saying, which I came across during my Boy Scout days in the Order of the Arrow: "Sometimes a man is not born to his home. He may find it elsewhere – later in his life – and he is at peace." I am at peace, Steven. I'm sure we'll have a chance to discuss this subject more deeply in the future. In the meantime, I thought I might catch you up on what's been keeping me so busy lately.

You remember I told you about the new housing project we're building here on the kibbutz? Well, it's really starting to take shape now, and within a month or two, we hope to begin construction of the first phase – ten small houses for young couples who would like to share in our good fortune and raise their families in the clean, fresh mountain air we have enjoyed for so many years.

The houses will be built so that they look out onto the extraordinary view of our mountain – Mount Hermon – the one you liked in the photograph I sent you a while back. As the sun rises over its lower peaks and illuminates the pastoral valley below, we feel truly blessed that we wake up each morning to one of Mother Nature's most beautiful gifts. And as evening draws near and the sun sets in the western sky, its rays throw such an array of colorful hues onto the mountain's face, that it would be a challenge to any artist's palette.

I'm enclosing an architect's rendering of the houses we're building. As you can see, they're simple two-story cottages, but with a great view! We've been interviewing many young couples who have shown an interest in joining our community, but not all are suited for the rural conditions of an isolated mountain community such as ours.

I'm sure you can understand now why I just don't have the time right now to take a trip to the States. But I'll get there one of these days. I promise!

Love,

Grandpa

Courtesy: Kibbutz Misgav-Am

February 23, 1998

Mr. Yoram Friedman
c/o Kibbutz Misgav-Am
Upper Galilee
Israel

Dad,

Steven was so enthralled with the way you described the kibbutz and its environs that he shared a portion of your last letter with Joan and me. We are pleased that you and Steven have found a common language. He really enjoys your correspondence. We think that having his grandfather as a pen pal can be a wonderful experience for him, but our only concern (and limitation) is that you steer clear of discussing Zionism, as you have done so far.

Hope you are well. Joan sends her best.
Michael

February 25, 1998

Dear Grandpa,

Your letters are so beautiful. The way you tell about the scenery is so nice that I just had to read that part of your letter to Mom and Dad. They thought it was pretty, too. They also reminded me not to ask you any ideology or politics questions about Israel, so I'll try not to, even though I don't exactly understand what ideology is, but it's hard because your country is always in the news on TV, with fighting and bombs and stuff, and I want to know what you think about it. I hope you are safe where you live, up in the mountains.

Grandpa, what you told me to do about Barbara I did, even

before I got your letter, and it worked. One day we were talking about our algebra homework before class, and I asked her if she would like to go to the movies sometime with me, or something, and she said yes. We didn't go to the movies, because nothing was playing that we both wanted to see, so we walked around the mall and talked. We discussed all sorts of things. I told her about you living in Israel, which really interested her. She's Protestant, but her family isn't religious, like ours isn't. We talked about my being Jewish, too. I told her about my bar mitzvah, and learning to read Hebrew and getting up on the pulpit to do my *haftora*, and then about the big party afterwards. She lives pretty close to me, so I walked her home and I met her mother, who is very nice too. When a good movie comes to the mall, we're going to go together. So it all seemed pretty natural. What a relief.

Grandpa, please send me a picture of how you look now. All I have is that picture of you on the Appalachian Trail when you were 15 years old, and I've seen some old photographs of you and Grandma in an album up in the attic. There are some extra bar mitzvah pictures of me, so Dad said I could send you one or two. I hope you like them. Please write soon.

Love,
  Steven

March 24, 1998

Dear Steven,

I was very pleased to read in your last letter that you enjoyed my writing so much that you shared a portion of my letter with your parents. You also express yourself very well, and I enjoy your letters immensely.

Even with all the problems we face here in Israel (as you noted in your last letter), I feel very blessed to be living in such a beautiful spot on this planet. And just to set your mind at ease, we are quite safe up here in our little mountain village.

I was also pleased to hear that you and Barbara enjoyed yourselves at the mall. At this point in your life it really doesn't matter if she's Jewish, Christian or Hindu. If you enjoy each other's company, and like talking to one another, that's what counts.

And now, having said that, I think it's about time I introduced you to *my* life's companion. My wife's name is Sarah, but everyone on the kibbutz calls her Saraleh (an affectionate nickname). We will be celebrating our fifteenth wedding anniversary next month. I'm enclosing a snapshot of the two of us on vacation in the south of the country (the Negev) last summer. She is a kindergarten teacher here on the kibbutz.

Saraleh is also a mom and a grandma. Her daughter Tami is married and they have two girls – Yael, who's your age, and Ronit, who's ten. Tami is a social worker; her husband Avi works for a small hi-tech firm in Kiryat Shmona, the provincial capital of northern Israel. Tami and Avi built their house just on the edge of town and we come down from our mountain to visit with them, and they usually come up to the kibbutz for Friday night dinner, and most of the holidays, as well. Kibbutz members used to have all their meals in a communal dining hall, but today families eat most meals at home. Saraleh's a great cook!

Steven, your bar mitzvah pictures are really wonderful. I've already had them framed. One of them is sitting on the living room buffet, along with pictures of Yael and Ronit, and the other is on my desk at work.

I hope the picture of Saraleh and me, which I'm enclosing with this letter, gives you the chance to see what your pen pal grandpa looks like, along with my lovely wife. My warmest regards to your folks.

Love,
Grandpa

April 18, 1998

Dear Grandpa,

I was really surprised (and happy) that you're married, and that you have a family in Israel. I don't know why I thought you lived alone, like Grandma. Your wife looks real nice in the picture you sent me, and so do you. You look younger than I thought, too, and I think it's really cool that you have a ponytail. My dad is bald! I don't know how that can be, that you have all your hair and my dad doesn't.

Grandpa, I know I'm not supposed to ask you this, but I think about it a lot, because we're friends now. Why did Grandma and Dad decide to move back to the States and you decided to stay in Israel? I know it was a long time ago, when Dad was a boy, but I'd really like to know. It's like this family secret that nobody wants to talk about. Barbara and I discussed it, and we think it's probably got something to do with politics and ideology, which you and I are not supposed to talk about. I like talking to Barbara about lots of things. She's really nice and *intelligent*.

Please send me pictures of your whole family. I feel like I have two new cousins that I never knew I had. I have two cousins here in the States too from Mom's side of the family. Mom's brother, Uncle Bob and his wife Aunt Sue have two boys. Matt is eight and Josh is five.

Please write soon.

Love,

Steven

May 7, 1998

Dear Steven,

Just to clear up the mystery of your father's baldness and my own "flowing locks," I believe that particular gene is passed down on the mother's side. I remember that your grandma's father lost his hair at an early age. If your mom's father still has his hair, then I believe you have a good chance for a full head of hair throughout your long lifetime – "until 120." (That's an expression we use here in Israel when we want to wish our loved ones a long and healthy lifetime.)

Now on to your next and more sensitive query about our family's history, and how we ended up living so many thousands of miles apart.

Steven, I really don't believe in family secrets and yet on the other hand, I can truly understand your father's reasons for not wanting to speak about or discuss our family's emotional break-up so many years ago. It was a wrenching decision for your grandma and me. Your dad, who was only fourteen at the time, suffered greatly because of that decision. Even though he may not appreciate my sharing the story with you now, I've decided to tell you the facts, as I remember them, without dwelling on the tremendous emotional upheaval we all went through at the time. I think you're old enough to understand both points of view and the decisions that were made at the time.

Please give your dad this letter to read. It's very important, Steven, that he knows I've shared this "family secret" with you. It shall be a "secret" no longer! I hope your dad shares my opinion that it would be best for you to understand our family history, and allows us to continue being pen pals.

In 1970, your grandmother and I, and our ten-year-old son (your dad) moved to Israel in the euphoric aftermath of the Six Day War. (That was a war between Israel and her Arab neighbors in June 1967.) We spent a brief period in what they call an "absorption center." Then we decided to live on a kibbutz, rather than the city, since it seemed to be a healthy and less stressful lifestyle for new immigrants like ourselves.

After searching from the Negev in the south to the Galilee in the north, we settled on Kibbutz Misgav-Am on Israel's northern frontier with Lebanon and Syria. The beauty of the area, with its incredible panoramic views, enthralled your grandma and me and quickly overshadowed any doubts we might have had about our safety. In fact, it blurred the geographic reality of where we were about to make our home.

Your Dad quickly adjusted to living separately from us in a "children's house," with boys and girls of his own age, under adult supervision, of course. They became his extended family of brothers and sisters. This was the kibbutz way. As I recall, your grandma and I had a pretty hard time adjusting to that arrangement. But your dad seemed pretty happy with his new extended family and, as time passed, we all settled into a rather nice, quiet and unique lifestyle, although those first couple of years as new immigrants were difficult for all of us. We had to adapt to the ways of the kibbutz. In the States I had been an architect, but in Israel, to my own amazement, I decided to become a farmer – and a fish farmer at that! Grandma, who had been an elementary school teacher before we moved to Israel, became a pre-school teacher (three to four year olds) and she loved it. Even though she was just beginning to learn Hebrew, she found many different ways to communicate with children of that age.

My own Hebrew was progressing slowly and Grandma and I were making new friends and beginning to feel a real part of our new community. Everything was starting to seem more normal to us. But then, without warning, earthshaking events occurred that not only altered the history of Israel and the entire Middle East, but also impacted on our little family – and continue to do so until this day!

In early October of 1973, our sense of "normalcy" was shattered – dramatically! At around two o'clock in the afternoon on October 6 (Yom Kippur), a Syrian warplane flew menacingly above our kibbutz, signaling the beginning of what would be called "The Yom Kippur War." Simultaneous surprise attacks by the Syrian Army in the north and the Egyptian Army in the south began the most difficult and costly war of the modern State of Israel, and it happened literally on our doorstep – within sight and sound. I can *still* "see and hear" the ferocious tank battles on the Golan Heights, directly across the valley from our kibbutz.

The trauma of that war, although historically a victory for Israel, forever changed the arrogant complacency of the Israeli government and the Israel Defense Forces (IDF). Unfortunately, many idealistic new immigrants (especially from the United States) had moved to Israel thinking that the victorious Six Day War in 1967 would discourage any Arab country from ever trying to destroy Israel again. They were wrong! Even as a fragile cease-fire was negotiated by the UN (under the watchful eyes of the Americans and the Soviets), the agonizingly difficult negotiations on prisoner exchanges and final disengagement lines lasted for months. And, our kibbutz was on the front line all this time.

For almost six months the children of our kibbutz and their teachers (including Grandma), ate, slept, studied and played in underground bomb shelters that were (and still are) scattered around our kibbutz like underground caves. Although these underground living quarters had electricity, plumbing, telephone lines and even black-and-white televisions with lots of cartoons for younger kids, it was a pretty difficult time for both the children and their adult guardians.

All the older men on the kibbutz (like me) took turns guarding the perimeter fence of our small mountain enclave, day and night. We also had to work extra-long hours in the fields, orchards and the fishponds, since all our younger men were on the front lines. They fought the enemy with tanks, planes and even hand-to-hand combat on the slopes and treacherous ascent to the peaks of Mount Hermon. We had to maintain our control of the high ground, no matter what the cost!

Those six months seem surrealistic now – almost twenty-five years later. But back then, it was all too real, and it took its toll on everyone, including Grandma and me. When the uneasy cease-fire finally turned into a workable truce with Egypt and Syria, our kibbutz gradually awoke from its "hibernation" and began to function normally again, not having to worry (at least not for the moment) that air-raid sirens would again blast out their scary wail, sending us scurrying back to the relative safety (albeit discomfort) of our underground shelters.

When the "smoke finally cleared" from that horrible war, over two thousand of our soldiers had been killed and many more thousands wounded and maimed. It had been a war like no other in our short history, and the entire country seemed to be in a daze from the psychological aftershocks which have lasted for years – even till this day!

Whatever the reasons, grandma and I reacted very differently to that prolonged state of emergency. My reaction to the war and its aftermath *reinforced* my ties to this land and to our kibbutz, as well as my unshakable belief that moving to Israel had been the right decision – even with the hardships we had endured so soon after our arrival. I felt truly at home in my adopted country and assumed that my wife and son felt the same. I was wrong! Grandma had spent nearly half a year living with and caring for the young children in her charge. It had been a daunting task – and had taken its toll.

By the fall of 1974, as our lives on the kibbutz returned to a semblance of normalcy, Grandma raised the idea of returning to the States to live. At first, I was in a state of complete shock and disbelief. Grandma had made so many friends here on the kibbutz; she was liked and respected by everyone. The children adored her. I couldn't understand her utter disillusionment with our dream of settling in the modern State of Israel, of being twentieth-century pioneers, helping to rebuild our homeland after 2000 years of exile.

Then she told me that she had spoken to our son about returning to America – and that he had agreed. I was devastated beyond consolation. When I confronted your Dad, he begged me to return with them to the States. "You're still an American!" he said, trying desperately to convince me to go back with him and grandma. "You could get your old job back with that big architectural firm you used to work for," he pleaded. He just didn't understand my total commitment to living in Israel. I was adamant about staying, and alternatively, I pleaded with him to stay – but to no avail.

Soon after the High Holidays in the fall of 1974, your dad and Grandma traveled to the airport, by themselves, and flew back to America – without me. I was very, very angry at the time. We were all angry. Your Dad felt (and probably still does) that I had deserted him and his mom. I felt the same, but with roles reversed – that my family was deserting me. I haven't spoken to your dad or to your Grandma ever since, although I have written each of them from time to time – with no response.

And so, Steven, that's the "family secret" that no one wants to talk about. The feeling of rejection on both sides runs very, very deep and has lasted for almost a quarter of a century. Maybe, somehow, you and I can heal those old wounds of misunderstanding and disappointment through our pen pal relationship. I hope so!

Love,

Grandpa

May 19, 1998

Mr. Yoram Friedman
c/o Kibbutz Misgav-Am
Upper Galilee, Israel

How dare you involve your thirteen-year-old grandson in the emotional trauma that you put Mom and me through so many years ago? Are you out of your mind? He's only a boy! I have forbidden Steven to continue your correspondence. Any letters you write to him will be returned unopened. Do I make myself clear?

Michael.

Part II

Three-and-a-half years later…
Shortly after 9/11

September 23, 2001

Mr. Yoram Friedman
c/o Kibbutz Misgav-Am
Upper Galilee, Israel

Dear Grandpa,

I've wanted to write to you for a long, long time, but you remember what happened after you wrote that serious letter to me about our family secret. Dad was very angry for a long time and he made me stop writing to you. I was only thirteen then. I wanted to write to you many times since. Now that I'm sixteen I've decided to go ahead and write to you, especially now, after what happened to us here in New York City and in Washington DC on September 11th.

The terrorist attack on the World Trade Center and the Pentagon is the worst thing that's ever happened in my whole life. That day, my teacher turned on the television in our classroom and we just watched all day long. Some of the girls cried, which I felt like doing too, but I didn't.

I still can't believe it really happened. When they showed people jumping out of the windows from the high floors of the buildings, some of the girls ran out of the room screaming. They just couldn't watch it anymore. I couldn't *stop* watching. It was like one of those Arnold Schwarzenegger or Bruce Willis movies, only no one stopped the bad guys from carrying out their horrible plan. All the while I was watching, I couldn't help thinking about you in

Israel and the buses being blown up and the restaurants and coffee houses being bombed. It's all on TV here in the States and I worry so much about you.

I wanted to write to you last year when all that fighting started again after those peace talks in Camp David broke down, but Dad still wouldn't let me. Now I'm sixteen. I have a junior driver's license and I'm getting my adult license this November when I turn seventeen. This time I told my Dad that I'm going to write to you anyway and that I'm very sorry if he doesn't approve. To my surprise, he said it was okay. I guess the shock of what's happened to us here in the States changed the way he feels.

Everyone's still in shock. How could this have happened to us? Why weren't we prepared? President Bush said that we're going to catch the terrorists who planned the attack and stop them from carrying out any more attacks on America. I hope he's right!

Before I sign off, I just wanted to tell you that I made "Eagle" when I was fifteen and last summer at Camp Leni-Lenopee, I was inducted into the Order of the Arrow – just like you, Grandpa. *"Wamapdendink W.W."* Do you remember?

Lots more to talk about, like hiking on the Appalachian Trail and canoe trips down the Delaware River etc. but I'll sign off for now,

Love,

Steven

P.S. Please write soon. Dad said he wouldn't interfere.

October 5, 2001

Dear Steven,

I'm so glad that you wrote to me. I also wanted to write to you as well, but I had to respect your father's wishes – as did you. I'm only sorry that it took this horrible national tragedy to give us the impetus to resume our pen pal relationship after more than three years. I missed you. But I'm not sorry I told you that story. You had to know. But let's not dwell on the past. The present is more than enough to digest.

Steven, I saw the same horrific television images as you and your classmates did, in real time, courtesy of CNN, and I have to tell you that it was the worst single event that I've ever witnessed in *my* lifetime as well. And I'm a little older than you. Terrorism has now become a global threat; I never imagined that the intended target of these terror attacks would be western civilization itself. But they're not going to win! The world has been given a horrible wake-up call. The United States and her allies (Israel is one of the staunchest among them) will, in time, overcome this new threat, just as good has always triumphed over evil in the long history of our civilized world. I know that there are difficult times ahead, but in the words of that inspirational Civil Rights song of the '60s, "We *shall* overcome!"

Steven, I'm so proud of you. You made "Eagle" at fifteen, just like your grandpa did some fifty+ years ago. It seems as though it was just yesterday. Please tell me all about the awards ceremony in your next letter. And, as if your attaining Eagle Scout weren't enough to have me bursting with pride, you and I are not only grandfather and grandson, but we have become "blood brothers" with your induction into the Order of the Arrow. Of course I remember! "*Wamapdendink – Win****sit – Wid*****oee*[1]" – ie. "Cheerful service to our fellow man." And I hope that someday we'll have a chance to use the secret handshake as well – along with a big hug.

Steven, it's been three years! We've got a lot of catching up to do. I'd really love to hear about your camping trips. You mentioned the Appalachian Trail and canoe trips down the Delaware River. I'd also like to hear about your plans and dreams for your future. Next year you'll be a senior in high school. Have you any thoughts about which college you'd like to attend? And what field interests

---

1. Author's note: Honoring lifetime oath of secrecy.

you as a possible career? Oh… and do you still see Barbara, your first girlfriend? And what ever happened with the swimming team? I remember you told me you were going to compete in the "butterfly" stroke. There's so much I'd like to know about your life during these past three years. Please try and fill me in on what's happened in your life since we last corresponded. I've missed my pen pal from New Jersey!

Saraleh and the kids send their best. Looking forward to your next letter.

Love,
Grandpa

October 23, 2001

Dear Grandpa,

I'm so glad you wrote back right away. I'd really missed writing you and receiving your letters. It's something that just you and I share.

I want you to know that I really love Mom and Dad. They're great parents, but I feel that I'm different from them – really different. You and I, though, are the same. I just feel it. We're like soul mates. I know I can tell you what I'm really feeling, and I know you'll understand. In your letter you mentioned "catching up," so first I'll tell you what I've been doing these last three years.

First of all, I made the swimming team my freshman year in high school. My personal best so far in the 100-meter butterfly is 1:01.53. It's not exactly Olympic qualifying time, but I'm getting close to my goal of breaking one minute. For me, it's like Roger Bannister's challenge of breaking the 4-minute mile. He did it back in 1954 and I know I'm going to break my one-minute barrier during this season. I'll let you know as soon as it happens!

My grades in school are okay. I've got a B+ average and my

parents want me to apply to Ivy League schools like Cornell, Yale, Princeton or even Harvard. I've got a real problem with that. Even though I told them I don't know yet what profession I want to go into, I really do! I want to apply to the University of Colorado, at Boulder, to study forestry. I can't tell them because they'll think I'm crazy and won't let me. Mom and Dad "tolerate" my outdoor activities, but I know they'll flip when they find out that I want to make it my profession. I know you understand but I'm sure they won't.

I don't know what to do. I know what they'll say when they find out: "That's not a profession for a nice Jewish boy!" They've got this Jewish snob thing. To them, it's like we're different or something. I don't understand them and they really don't understand me.

I remember you once told me that your parents didn't understand your love of the outdoors either, but they finally let you go. Well, it's been the same with me. Camping and hiking has been my life for these past three to four years. Mom and Dad put up with my somewhat unconventional activities because I'm a good student and they have no excuse to say no. I'm just not cut out to be a lawyer or a doctor or an engineer. I really want to be a forest ranger.

By the way, I hope you won't be disappointed, but for the time being, I've dropped out of Scouts. I was senior patrol leader for a whole year, with a lot of responsibility for the whole troop. What I really want to do is just go camping and hiking with my friends from other troops who enjoy the outdoors as much as I do.

I haven't told my parents yet, but my camping buddies and I have been making plans for this coming summer vacation. We want to take a train or bus up to Maine and spend a week or two hiking southward from Mount Katadin, the northern starting point of the Appalachian Trail. Did you ever hike in Maine?

Someday I'd like to hike the whole trail from Mount Katadin in Maine to Mount Oglethorpe in Georgia. I found an old issue of *National Geographic* magazine with the story of this college professor who took a year's leave of absence and hiked the whole trail – over

2,000 miles. He wore out 10 pairs of hiking boots! The pictures of his year's adventure were fantastic. I really liked his photographs of the Blue Ridge Mountains of Kentucky and Virginia. They're really beautiful. I hope to see them in person someday.

Anyway, there are five of us from all over New Jersey who sort of bonded when Pappi introduced us at Camp Leni-Lenopee a few summers ago. We hike together on the ⚑. We're sort of like this exclusive band of hikers. It's really cool! My parents finally realized that I know how to take care of myself in the woods (even in winter), so on long weekends and holidays like Thanksgiving, Christmas/Hanukah and Easter, they just sort of gave in to my need for outdoor adventure. My Dad always gives me his cell-phone with an extra battery in case of an emergency.

Of course, my hiking buddies and I also hook up over the summers at camp. We've hiked on the Trail in New Jersey, New York State and Pennsylvania – up near Tri-State Park, near the Delaware Water Gap. Do you remember that area? It's incredibly beautiful! We've also canoed on the Delaware from Port Jervis southward. Didn't you canoe on that stretch of river?

Pappi got married and now that he and his wife have a baby, he can't get away like he used to – not even in the summer. We all miss him. He's a great camper and hiker and we learned a lot from him.

Oh yes, I still see Barbara. She's a really good friend, and we can talk about anything. We're also on the debating team together. But I go out with lots of girls now. I don't believe in going steady, although I have been tempted once or twice. I just don't have the time for that kind of thing. Between school, the swimming team, the debating club, and my outdoor activities, I'm all booked up! My parents already complain that I don't spend enough time with them.

Please say hi to your wife and whole family for me. Write soon!

Love,

    Steve

November 5, 2001

Dear Steven,

I just got your letter and I wanted to write you a quick note in time for your seventeenth birthday – *mazal tov!* You'll be getting your driver's license soon.

I also got my driver's license a week after my seventeenth birthday. I really have to give my parents a lot of credit – they let me take the car up to Camp Mohican the last weekend of that summer for the Order of the Arrow induction ceremony. I remember feeling both grown-up and frightened at the same time. It was a big responsibility to take the family car and drive over 100 miles to camp and back. My parents must have been worried sick. There were no cell-phones in those days, so I made one phone call when I got safely to camp – and that was it until I arrived home about eight o'clock on Sunday night. To tell you the truth, I don't know who was more relieved that I got home safely – my parents or me!

Your remarks concerning your future, i.e. university, forestry etc. have given me much to think about. I really do understand your feelings. I would, though, like to take a bit of time to put my thoughts together before addressing such an important issue as your future. I'll write again soon with more about that.

In the meantime Saraleh and I and your whole family on this side of the ocean want to wish you a very Happy Seventeenth Birthday.

Lots of love,
Grandpa

November 16, 2001

Dear Steven,

I finally managed to find a quiet hour or so to reflect upon, and to write you, some of my thoughts concerning your last letter – your college education, future profession etc. Steven, I want you to know that I'm probably the only person in your family who *does* understand your love and passion for the outdoors. Most logically, your interests indicate a future career with the U.S. Forestry Service. I know how difficult these decisions can be. Although you asked only for a sympathetic ear, and not for my advice, I do have some thoughts that I hope you might find helpful.

I think it's wise to take the SAT and whatever other college entrance exams are required today. Apply to as many universities as possible, including the Ivy League schools, as well as the University of Colorado. And... instead of that hiking trip up in Maine next summer, maybe you could volunteer your services to the New Jersey Forestry Service and see – firsthand – what it's all about.

I know you'll be accepted to one or more of those Ivy League schools, if you apply. Try out a semester or two. You don't have to stay. If forestry is your calling, it will make itself heard, loud and clear! And last but not least... You don't have to pay attention to any of the above. My feelings won't be hurt.

Steven, considering our mutual love of the outdoors, you probably won't be surprised to learn that I also considered forestry as a possible profession. But then, later in my teens, I read a book by Ayn Rand entitled *The Fountainhead*, which loosely portrayed the life and career of Frank Lloyd Wright, the great American architect and idealist. I began to look at houses, buildings, and structures in general with a different and more discerning eye. And when I saw photographs of Wright's masterpiece, "Falling Water" – a house in the woods near Bear Run, Pennsylvania, with cantilevered balconies jutting out dramatically over a beautiful waterfall – I was hooked. I was going to be an architect!

Still, when I graduated from high school, I felt conflicted. I did have a talent for drawing and a love of the arts, but my other love, the great outdoors, was still beckoning me toward an adventurous career in forestry.

So... I decided I needed some time to think things through, a sort of break from the tensions of decision making. Much to the chagrin of my parents, I took an extended "break" – three years in the U.S. Army! – and I had *lots* of time to "think things through." I ended up in Occupied Germany, facing off the Red Army of the former Soviet Union – tank to tank, soldier to soldier, in the early years of the Cold War. Thank God hostilities never broke out, but we did have some "hairy" moments, as I recall.

When I finished my tour of duty, I finally decided on a career in architecture, and studied at the University of California at Berkeley. It turned out to be a wonderfully rewarding profession and I truly enjoyed my years as an architect.

But as fate would have it, when I made aliyah (moved to Israel) some years later, I returned to my first love – the great outdoors – albeit as a fish farmer on a kibbutz in northern Israel. So... what's my advice to you after my wordy reminiscences of my own decision-making process? – DON'T JOIN THE U.S. ARMY!

Seriously though, my most important message to you for the immediate future is – enjoy your last years in high school. No decision that you will make now is "carved in stone."

Now I want to take a moment to tell you what *I've* been up to these days. If you remember, in some of my letters of three years ago, I told you about my involvement in the new housing project we undertook here on the kibbutz. Well, Phase 1 – the first twenty units – is now complete. It has been my responsibility to interview the young couples who wish to live among us. Not everyone, of course, is suited to our rural lifestyle, never mind psychologically prepared to live on a border settlement that sits directly across from our enemies – although they all emphatically claim that they are. Over half the units are now occupied and, at the moment, we seem to have more applicants than available houses. Phase 2 of the project (ten more housing units) will be completed in another year –

we hope! Anyway, you can see that I keep myself pretty busy of late.

As a last thought Steven, life has a way of steering its own course. Enjoy the ride!

With love,

Grandpa

December 8, 2001

Dear Grandpa,

Thanks for the birthday wishes. Turning seventeen is sort of different than the other birthdays. I guess it's because I can drive now. I got my license last week. Dad said I can take the family car (a Ford Taurus) on either Friday or Saturday nights and once in a while to swimming practice during the week. I also have to wash it and maybe wax it now and then. Dad's private car is one of those off-road 4×4s (a Toyota Land Cruiser with a big diesel engine). I don't know why he bought such a powerful car. He and Mom wouldn't go camping in a million years. Their idea of a vacation is a luxury hotel up in the Catskills, and they've flown down to Bermuda a couple of times. I do my own thing, so we haven't taken a family vacation since I was a kid. I like it that way.

First of all, Happy Hanukah and Happy New Year too. I hope 2002 will be a better year for us (and for Israel). President Bush sent our troops to fight the Taliban in Afghanistan because that's where the Al-Qaeda terror organization trained. They're the ones that attacked the World Trade Center and the Pentagon. I think he was right to send our troops, but don't worry, I'm not going to join the army when I graduate high school, like you did.

Grandpa, after I read your last letter, I was really amazed at what an adventurous life you've had, especially when you were young. I also really admire you for making some tough decisions about your life and then following them through, even though it must have been hard sometimes. But I bet those years you spent in the army in Germany were pretty exciting. I'd like to hear more about that. You were in Germany pretty soon after World War II and the Holocaust. Did that have anything to do with your moving to Israel later on?

I also want to thank you for sending me your ideas about my own decisions about my future. I'm not exactly sure yet what I'm going to do, but thank you for your advice. I know you care about me and that makes me feel real good.

There has been one big change in my plans for next summer. Instead of my going up to Maine to hike on the ⚲, Mom and Dad have agreed to let me go for a month to the Boy Scout Summer Ranch out in Colorado. It's up in the mountains a few miles outside of the town of Glenwood Springs. Maybe you can look it up in an atlas. I've dreamt of going there ever since I joined the Scouts. They go backpacking and horseback trekking up into the mountains and they also teach a wilderness survival course. Pappi told me he learned most of his outdoors skills at the Ranch. In order to go, you have to be *in* the Scouts, so my hiking friends and I joined Pappi's old Explorer troop in Nutley. They're called "Venturer" Scouts now. We meet once a month.

A month on the ranch, including flights back and forth, is pretty expensive, but I guess Mom and Dad thought it would be better than having me wandering up in the mountains of Maine without supervision. We'll do the Maine trip the summer after graduation.

That's all for now. Write soon!

Love,

Steve

P.S. Everyone (except Mom and Dad) calls me Steve. Please call me Steve.
P.P.S. Grandpa, please be careful! I worry about you and those horrible things that happen in Israel. I hope you and your wife don't go on buses.

January 3, 2002

Dear Steve,

Sorry for the delay in writing, but as usual I've been really busy with my work, so much so that Saraleh and I decided to take a week's vacation in our southern sea-resort city of Eilat on the Gulf of Aqaba/Eilat.

Right now though, I want to tell you how excited I am for you about your plans for next summer at the Scout Ranch in Colorado. You are fulfilling a dream I myself had from the time I first heard about the ranch when I joined the Scouts. I never realized that dream, but I think you can imagine how I feel now, knowing my grandson is going to live those wonderful adventures in my stead. Even after all these years, I'll be able to trek those mountain passes with you – through your letters, of course. I hope you'll keep a journal; not only of your day-to-day experiences, but of your feelings as you witness the extraordinary splendor of America's western mountain range – the magnificent Rockies. It seems to me from your past letters (even when you were younger) that you have a special flair for writing. I really enjoy your letters and I hope you'll tell me more about your plans as the months pass and next summer draws nigh.

Saraleh and I enjoyed our Eilat vacation. Thank God we now have peaceful borders with Egypt and Jordan. Maybe someday we'll be able to finally sign peace treaties with Lebanon and Syria, our neighbors to the north, as well. However, before that happens, we have to come to some kind of solution to the Israeli/Palestinian conflict. And, *that* can only happen when the terror attacks on our civilian population stop. Neither we, nor any free people, should negotiate under the threat of terror.

Now that Israeli politics is no longer a taboo subject for our correspondence, we can discuss this in future letters – if you'd like. Which reminds me, I just wanted to mention how astute it was of you to make the connection between my military service in Occupied Germany and my moving to Israel (making aliyah) later in life. To answer your searching question – Did my experiences in Germany have anything to do with my moving to Israel? – the answer is yes, most definitely! It would take many letters to discuss the subject of aliyah, but since you asked, I thought I might attempt a beginning in this letter. The story begins almost a decade before I served with the American Army in Occupied West Germany.

When World War II ended in 1945, I was only ten years old. All I knew at the time was that we beat the Nazis and the "Japs" and that, since our soldiers were coming home, there wouldn't be any more families like our next-door neighbors, whose son was killed somewhere in Europe. At the Saturday afternoon matinees at the movies, they used to show newsreels (between the two main features) of soldiers embarking on the huge transport ships that would bring them home from Europe and the Pacific. The newsreels also showed our soldiers liberating so-called "camps" of civilian prisoners wearing striped clothes. And they showed lots and lots of dead bodies – grotesque piles of naked emaciated dead bodies.

And that would be the end of the newsreel. Then the main feature would begin and my friends and I would become engrossed in some Hollywood western or maybe even a heroic war film. Even though I was far too young to understand the significance of those horrific celluloid images, they somehow remained imprinted on my memory – till this day.

However, back then, all I could think about were my youthful activities, which changed direction significantly when I reached my twelfth birthday in 1947 and joined the Boy Scouts of America. Through my scouting activities, I was introduced to my lifetime love of the outdoors.

A year later, in 1948, two other significant events took place. The first was my bar mitzvah, which finally emancipated me from four years of mandatory Hebrew School. The second was taking place halfway around the world – the newly created Jewish State of

Israel was fighting its war of independence. I really didn't pay much attention to my parents' conversations about the rebirth of the Jewish State. What did that have to do with me? I was an American teenager emerging into the best years of my life.

Steve, if you're really interested, I'll continue the story of my metamorphosis over the following two decades, from a typical second-generation American (a liberal Democrat) into a political Zionist with a desire to live in the Jewish State. I'll include a paragraph or two in each of my letters, so that we can talk about lots of other things as well. In the meantime, enjoy your life and please keep writing me about your adventures. I really enjoy your letters.

Love,

Grandpa

January 18, 2002

Dear Grandpa,

Your letters are always so interesting and make me think of things I usually don't think about – and that's good! When I studied World War II in my history class, I remember the emphasis was on how the Allied victory affected the future of the world. The *Holocaust* was never mentioned!

For instance, we learned that in Europe, the end of the war led almost immediately into a new "Cold War" between East and West and the very real threat of mutual nuclear suicide. In the Far East, the victory over Japan affected the future of the world in a very different way. Within less than two decades after their total defeat in the war, the Japanese regained their status as a world superpower – though this time their goal was to dominate not other countries and peoples, but the world marketplace. Their work ethic, expertise in manufacturing, advertising and distribution of their products changed the world's economy in the second half of the twentieth century.

So other than the basic facts about the German and Japanese aggression against their regional neighbors (especially the Japanese attack on Pearl Harbor in December of 1941), the D-Day landing of the Allied Forces on the coast of France in June of 1944, and, of course, the A-bombing of Hiroshima and Nagasaki, the *aftermath* of World War II is what we studied – nothing about the Holocaust! Since I'm Jewish, I learned a little about the Holocaust at temple, in Hebrew school and at the JCC. But it wasn't until they showed Steven Spielberg's movie "Schindler's List" at our school assembly that I began to *feel* the Holocaust. It greatly affected me and my friends (even the non-Jewish ones). I think that the movie is being shown in all the high schools in the United States.

From my history lessons in Hebrew school, I remember that Theodor Herzl started the movement to establish a Jewish home-land in Palestine because of the persecution of Jews in Europe for hundreds of years. Then, during World War I, there was the "Bal-four Declaration" which said that the Jewish people should have their own land in Palestine. But it never actually happened until after World War II. I guess the world was so shocked at what the Nazis did to the Jews that they (the UN) finally decided in favor of the Jewish homeland. But then, all the fighting started with the Arabs and it's still going on.

What I really don't understand is why the Arabs are fighting over such a small country. There are so many Arab countries, and they're all rich because of their oil. I also don't understand why you went to live in Israel. You were born and raised in America and Jews in America are just like everyone else. There's no discrimina-tion against us. Why did you feel you had to move to Israel to be Jewish – or *more* Jewish than you were in the United States? I hope you'll try to explain because it will help me get to know you better, and I think it will also help me to better understand the differences between you and my Dad. I really want to understand.

Now back to our less serious topic of discussion – camping! My buddies and I are planning a trip to Tri-State Park during the long "Presidents' Birthdays" weekend next month (Washington and Lincoln got grouped together). Mom and Dad think we're all crazy because February in usually the coldest month of the year, but we love it – and we're prepared for the cold weather. My sleeping bag can keep me warm at -30° centigrade. I sent away for it from a camping supply company in Fairbanks, Alaska. I got my winter tent from them as well. It's the same kind that mountain climbers use when they try for the summit of Mount Everest or K-2 in the Himalayas. I hope it snows next month!

I just received the brochure and application for the Scout Ranch. The pictures are spectacular! We'll be going for the whole month of August. I'll write you all the details as the summer comes closer and of course I'll keep a journal of my adventures out west.

Please write soon. I really want you to continue your story of how you became a Zionist. Please say hi for me to your wife and whole family.

Love,

Steve

February 10, 2002

Dear Steve,

When this letter arrives, you'll probably be on that camping trip you wrote me about. I hope you're having a great time! I remember quite vividly how cozy it was, snuggled up in my eider down sleeping bag on a winter camping trip. But I can also remember how difficult it was to climb out in the morning and get dressed, especially putting on those frozen boots. Then someone taught me a great trick. At night, you just take your boots into the sleeping bag with you and in the morning they are as warm as toast.

Steve, you said in your last letter that you'd like me to continue writing about my personal journey toward Zionism. I'll be glad to. However, before I begin, I'd just like to clarify one historical fact.

On November 29th, 1947, the UN voted in favor of *partitioning* this tiny strip of land on the east coast of the Mediterranean, known as Palestine, into two separate independent states: one Jewish and one Arab. The Jews agreed, but the Arabs did not – leading to the bloody and bitter conflict that has lasted until this day. If you're interested in the chronology of the events in our region, I can send you several books that try to analyze our ongoing struggle in a (more or less) even-handed manner. I'm sure the Internet can also give you a general overview if you search for "The Israeli/Palestinian Conflict."

Now back to my own personal journey, which led me, some thirty-plus years ago, to leave the United States, the country of my birth, and join my own people in the extraordinary adventure of helping to rebuild the Jewish homeland in Israel. This momentous event was actually taking place in *my* lifetime (after two thousand years of Jewish exile from the land). There was simply no way that I was going to miss this opportunity to be a real participant in the history of the Jewish people. But that's getting way ahead of my story. Let's backtrack a bit to my own teenage years, growing up blissfully in Newark, New Jersey in the early 1950s.

My high school years were not all that different from your own. I went to Weequahic High School on Chancelor Ave. Maybe you've heard of it. It was quite prestigious in its day. Anyway, I kept my grades up just so my parents would allow me to go on my outdoor adventures. As I remember, I really enjoyed my high school years, but I didn't take many things seriously – especially my studies. They were just a means to an end, and that end was my next camping trip. Reading through your letters to me, you're much more academically oriented than I was at that time.

As a result, when it came time to continue my studies at the university level, I just wasn't ready. Much to my parents' chagrin, I volunteered for a three-year hitch in the U.S. Army. As fate would have it, the Korean War had just wound down to a very uneasy truce (which lasts till this day) and I was sent, not to Korea, but to

Occupied West Germany as part of the NATO forces facing off the Soviet Union and her Cold War allies.

As soon as I landed on German soil, those grotesque celluloid images from the Saturday afternoon matinees of a decade earlier reappeared before me, somehow making me aware that *this* was the place where it had all happened. That horrible newsreel footage had been taken somewhere here in Germany. I became obsessed with the idea of finding out from the local inhabitants if they were also haunted by the same images.

As I'm writing about these memories, I find myself becoming very emotional, so I'll stop here for the time being. I'll continue my story in a future letter. Please write to tell me about that weekend overnight. I hope it wasn't too cold. Regards to your folks.

Love,

Grandpa

February 13, 2002

Dear Steve,

I sent out my last letter to you just three days ago, but I feel compelled to continue writing about this segment of my journey without a time lapse, in order not to lose the momentum of expressing my emotions as I recall those impromptu confrontations with the "locals."

I would usually initiate an innocuous conversation with a German man who looked as if he was in his thirties or older. Since most of the populace spoke a simple, but understandable, broken English, I had no trouble communicating. I'd usually start off with innocent questions, even sympathetic. "What was it like here toward the end of the war?" "Was there enough food?" "How did everyone manage?" Then, when I had built up his confidence, I would ask the next obvious question: "And what did you do during the war?" No matter whom I spoke to, what age, farmer or teacher, laborer or restaurant owner, the answer was always the same, stated with great pride: "I fought on the Russian front – much fighting."

It seemed no one had ever fought the Americans or the British; they had always fought "those horrible Russians." But I guess that's a pretty understandable answer considering the circumstances, so I always played along with interest and sympathy toward whatever story they told me.

Then, after a few more amenities, I'd get around to asking about their religion. Were they Christian? Did they go to church? "Of course," was the universal answer, as they pointed in the direction of their local church or chapel. Then I'd say, with my finger tapping my chest, "I'm Jewish, I'm Jew...ish." There was always this inquisitive look, a blank stare of non-recognition. "I'm Jewish," I'd repeat, and then I would draw the Star of David on the ground with my finger or on a napkin if we were in a restaurant. Oh, yes, now they understood! "Jude, Jude" as they repeated their German pronunciation of "Jew."

The first time I heard that word I realized instantly that I had *seen* it before – somewhere. It must have been in one of those newsreel documentaries about Jewish refugees after the war. Then I remembered. It was printed in the middle of the yellow Star of David patch that all Jews were required to wear in Nazi Germany and occupied Europe during World War II – before they were led off to the death camps. I shuddered as the word was repeated once again: "Jude." They understood! "Did you know any Jews before the war?" I'd ask inquisitively, still maintaining my air of friendliness. "Nein, nein," came the predictable answer. "They lived in other cities."

Then I'd hit them with the big one. "Did they know what happened to the Jews during the war? Did they ever hear about those 'special camps' where Jews and Gypsies were taken?" By this time, my manner was no longer casual. I was deadly serious. I wanted an answer. I wanted someone to finally admit that they had known.

Someone had to have known! But their answer was always, "Nein, nein, I was on the Russian front for four years," and with that final declaration of their innocence and ignorance they would abruptly end the conversation and leave. Time after time, the same questions, the same answers and the same abrupt end. No one knew anything about the Jews, or the Gypsies, or the homosexuals, or the retarded people. They'd all just disappeared and no one knew anything about them, and obviously, no one cared.

My non-Jewish friends who were sometimes with me during these impromptu interrogations finally began to understand. Something monstrous had happened here. Something that we were all incapable of understanding. It was beyond our comprehension.

After I finished my two-year tour of overseas duty, I was shipped back to the States. I spent a short stint at Fort Riley, Kansas, where I was honorably discharged after serving my impulsive, yet worthwhile, three-year enlistment in the U.S. Army.

Steve, I hope my graphic recollections weren't too emotional. These memories are as vivid to me today as they were half a century ago. My experiences in Germany had changed me. I was no longer just an adventurous kid dreaming about his next camping trip. The very essence of who I *really* was, wasn't as simple as it used to be. I had always thought of myself as an American who just happened to be Jewish. Now I wondered: was I, in fact, a Jew who just happened to be born in America? And what was my connection to those European Jews who were slaughtered by the Nazis in their "ethnic cleansing" of Europe? Those were the questions I grappled with as I re-emerged into civilian life; no longer a boy, but a young adult finally ready to seek a proper education and take my place as a contributing member of American society.

That's all for now. I guess it's been quite a lot to digest. I hope not too much.

Love,
Grandpa

March 3, 2002

Dear Grandpa,

I received both your letters and before I start this letter, I just wanted to thank you for that great tip about the boots. Even Pappi never taught us that one. If we go on another overnight this winter, I'll try it out. But the weather's starting to get a little warmer already. It's probably because of the "global warming" everyone is talking about.

Anyway, we had a great time up at Tri-State over the holiday weekend. The weather was great and if you remember, the views are fantastic. We always seem to meet interesting people while we're on the trail or at campsites. This time we met a math professor from Princeton and his family. His wife runs a plant nursery on the outskirts of town and they have two great kids who help out their mom at the nursery. We were camped right next to them and we got along so well that they invited Joel and me to join them for supper one night. We didn't have anything else to bring, so I whipped up a batch of my special camping stew. You take chunks of dried meat, potatoes, carrots etc., add salt and pepper and a bit of water, wrap it up tight in tin foil, and then you throw the whole package into the hot coals for about half an hour. When you open it up, all the juices from the meat and vegetables make a great gravy. Everybody loved it – including the kids. They served us steaks, home fries, more vegetables and for dessert we had the best lemon meringue pie I ever tasted.

We talked about lots of things – even about you. They were very interested and thought it was very unusual and special that you chose to live out your ideals, even at great personal sacrifice. So do I, Grandpa. They were obviously not Jewish, so I didn't talk about any of the things you wrote me about in your last two letters. It just didn't seem appropriate to discuss such an emotional subject with strangers. I don't even want to talk about it with Mom and Dad – just you, at least for now.

I've read and re-read your last two letters over and over again.

The first thing I thought about when I read the first letter was that fate seems to have played a strange role in steering the direction of your life. If you had chosen to be a more serious student in high school, your life would have been completely different. Also, if the Korean War would have gone on a few more months, you might have been sent there instead of Germany. Thank God you weren't!

My feelings as I read and re-read your second letter (many, many times) are difficult to describe. It was an extremely emotional experience for me to be a *vicarious* (I just learned that word) witness to those conversations – or should I say "interrogations" – of more than half a century ago.

As I said once before, your letters make me think about things I usually don't think about. This time, it's the Nazi genocide of 6 million Jews. Not only is that difficult for me to comprehend, but it is impossible to understand the hate which motivated such a horrible atrocity. As I was reading each line of your dialogue with those "silent witnesses," I began to feel like I was there with you when you confronted them.

Grandpa, you were only a little older than me at the time. How did you have the courage to do what you did? Whatever it was, it seems to have started a change within yourself that you probably weren't even aware of at the time. The direction of your life was different from then on.

Grandpa, thank you for sharing this story with me. For the first time since our correspondence began, I'm beginning to understand some of the events in your life that helped to shape who you are today. Please continue with your story (along with other things too) so that I can get to know you better. Maybe someday I'll be able to help make peace between you and my Dad. I hope so! Now, I'm off to play some basketball with my friends. I didn't make the varsity team at school, but I love the game.

Love,

Steve

March 18, 2002

Dear Steve,

I've also read and re-read your response to my last two letters. After I mailed them, I had second thoughts about what I had written. I was concerned that I might have been too emotional in expressing my recollection of events that took place so long ago. But then I realized I couldn't have begun my story in any other way – emotions and all. When I received your last letter, I knew I truly had a pen pal with whom I could share many things; not just pleasantries like our mutual love of the outdoors, but other more personal things that dig deep into one's soul. The fact that you're my grandson makes our pen pal relationship that much more satisfying and rewarding for me.

I remember the last time I wrote to you with such passion. You were much younger then, and your Dad *rightfully* stopped our correspondence. I was wrong, Steve. I should not have burdened you with such a "heavy" story about our family history. Even though you asked me to tell you, I should have waited till you were older. Although it took the unthinkable calamity of 9/11 to get our words flowing again, I'm sure it would have happened anyway – when the time was right. And it seems the time is certainly right – now!

I mentioned once before that I think you're quite perceptive. You picked up immediately on the strange role fate seems to have played in steering the course of my young life. I would take it even a step further. Not every Jewish soldier who served in Occupied Germany after the war was affected as I was. Why was I selected to feel so deeply the subliminal "smoke and ashes" of the horror that had occurred on that soil a decade before my arrival? Why was I compelled to investigate the past, and to interrogate the witnesses and maybe even the perpetrators of a crime against their fellow human beings that was so unthinkable, it would henceforth be referred to in the history of modern civilization as "The Holocaust."

After those bizarre encounters with the "locals" my life was never the same. Those experiences began a series of events in my life that eventually led me – many years later – to leave the shores of the American dream, in order to participate in another dream – the rebuilding of the Jewish homeland in Israel.

But again, as usual, I'm getting way ahead of my story. Let's get back to those delightfully innocent days in America (the '50s) when the key to success, both professionally and socially was – assimilation.

Even with my unique experiences while serving with the U.S. Army in Germany, I was neither old enough nor wise enough to know what to do with what I had learned. And so, like most of my Jewish contemporaries of the time, I also followed that "yellow brick road" called assimilation toward its promised reward of success – American style; I more or less achieved that success after completing a proper education and joining the American work force. That was around the time I met your Grandma. We met at the JCC in San Francisco, fell in love and were married soon afterwards. Your Dad came along in due course, and that was our little family. And on that note of genealogy, I think I'll take a break from my personal saga and get back to more down-to-earth subjects like that camping stew you wrote me about.

Steve, that's got to be the oldest camping recipe around! We made that same stew back when I was in the Scouts! We used the same lightweight dried food that mountain climbers used. Your stories bring back such wonderful memories for me, although I have to say (in retrospect) that those dried foods weren't all that great. They just seemed to taste so terrific when we were out on the trail. With all the modern food technology of today, I hope they're making some better-tasting concentrated foods, especially for the astronauts who are up in space at the International Space Station, sometimes for months at a time.

It's getting late, so I'll sign off for now. Saraleh joins me in sending you and your folks wishes for a very happy Passover.

Love,

Grandpa

TERROR STRIKES PASSOVER SEDER
Dateline: March 27, 2002 – Netanya, Israel.

By 7:30 PM the main dining room of the Park Hotel was filled to capacity with religious families who chose to spend the Passover holiday at this luxurious seaside hotel here in Netanya. The in-house rabbi had just begun leading everyone in the traditional reading of the Haggada.

As each family, some three generations strong, read in unison, a stranger somehow slipped past the security guard in the lobby and – unnoticed – made his way to the festivities. Shouting out the infamous words "Allahu Akbar" (God is the greatest, in Arabic) above the rhythmic hum of the readers, the man blew himself up, creating a huge explosion that engulfed the entire hall, killing over twenty people and maiming dozens more. Another suicide bomber had brought terror and bloodshed to the Jewish people, this time in the midst of their Passover Seder – a celebration of the exodus from Egypt and freedom from slavery over three thousand years ago.

*   *   *

Within minutes of this latest terror attack in Israel, international TV networks broadcast the grisly details across the globe and into the living rooms of hundreds of millions of people – including the Friedman family of Livingston, New Jersey. Steve felt he had to call his grandfather in Israel and talk to him about this horrible attack. A letter just wouldn't do!

"Hello..."

"Ah… Hello, is this the Friedman residence?"

"Yes… Who is this?," Sareleh asked in her hesitant English, taken aback a bit by the youthful English-speaking voice on the other end of the line.

"Hi… This is Steve from New Jersey. Can I speak to my Grandpa, please?"

"Oh, hello… yes, of course… just a minute," Sareleh exclaimed in quick succession, flustered for a moment with excitement. Yoram's grandson was actually calling from America… for the very first time!

"Yoram, come quick… it's your grandson from America!," she yelled out excitedly, switching back automatically into her native Hebrew.

"Really?… Hello Steve, is that you?"

"Yes, Grandpa! How are you?"

"I'm fine… and how are you? Is everything all right?"

"Oh… yes, everything's okay Grandpa, but I just had to call you about what happened yesterday. It was really horrible! We saw it all on CNN. How could somebody blow himself up like that? And they do it on buses too… and in shopping malls! These suicide attacks have been going on for over a year now. How can Israelis live like that? Aren't you afraid to go out?"

"Of course we're afraid, Steve. But we have to go on with our lives; we can't let these terrorists win in *any way*. If we have to hide in our homes, afraid to go out, then they've won. Our security forces have prevented hundreds and hundreds of attacks, but every now and then a terrorist gets through. And then, the whole country mourns with the families who have lost loved ones in these insane suicide attacks. This attack hit us all especially hard because it happened during a Passover Seder."

"I know, Grandpa. We feel it too. Even Mom and Dad couldn't stop watching the news. Grandpa, I'm really sorry our first telephone call was about this, but I just had to call you."

"I'm sorry too, Steve, but I'm really glad you called. Both our countries are at war now. A war against terror. And we will win – both of us!"

"I know, Grandpa. It was great hearing your voice. Mom and Dad say hi."

"Send them my best, and a happy Passover holiday."

"Okay, Grandpa. Write soon, okay?"

"You too. Thanks for calling. Bye!"

"Bye, Grandpa!"

April 6, 2002

Dear Grandpa,

The week of Passover is over now, but the memory of that suicide attack in Israel on Seder night is still very much in my mind. CNN and some other news stations showed those horrible pictures on TV for days afterwards. When I told Dad I just had to talk to you on the phone, he surprised me by agreeing without an argument. I guess 9/11 changed a lot of things – even Dad. Maybe someday you and Dad will be able to talk again. I hope so.

President Bush has already sent our troops to Afghanistan to fight the Taliban and Al-Qaeda terrorists. The new century is just beginning and already we're at war. I was thinking about the last century and trying to remember all the wars we studied about in Modern History class. First there were World Wars I and II, then Korea and Vietnam (both French and American), Bosnia/Serbia, the horrible tribal wars of Africa, the fifty-year-long "Cold War" between East and West, the Gulf War with Iraq and, of course, the many wars Israel has fought since 1948. Oh, and I almost forgot the war England fought with Argentina over the Falkland Islands. I'm sure there were more bloody battles around the world that I've forgotten about or we somehow skipped over, but the ones I've mentioned stand out in my mind.

It was a pretty horrible century as far as war is concerned, but it was also an amazing century from a technical point of view. We went from the Wright Brothers' first plane flight to landing on the moon in a rocket ship. We went from the mechanical age to the computer age and the most incredible thing of all (to my mind, at least) – we have actually counted and mapped out all the genes in the human body. Isn't that amazing? It's both exciting and scary at the same time.

I hope we know what to do with all this information. Those experiments in cloning are really weird. What mad scientist ever thought of such a thing in the first place? If they stick to sheep and pigs for medical research I guess it's okay, but what about the future? Will another mad scientist try and clone a human being? And then what?

That's enough serious talk for a while. I've got some great news to tell you. Mom and Dad have agreed to let me fly to Colorado a week before our session begins at the Scout Ranch, in order to check out the School of Forestry at the University of Colorado. Isn't that amazing? I guess my being on the debating team at school has had some practical side benefits; apparently my persuasive skills have improved – even with Mom and Dad! I'll be flying to Colorado the last week in July. I've already contacted the university and they'll be expecting me. I'm really excited, as you can imagine.

Grandpa, it was great hearing your voice on the phone. Your wife sounds really nice too. I'm only sorry our first telephone call was about such a horrible thing. Please write soon.

Love,
    Steve

April 18, 2002

Dear Steve,

I'm so pleased to hear that your parents are allowing you to investigate a possible career in forestry, vis-à-vis the University of Colorado. That's a real sign of their confidence and respect for your judgment and considerations about the future. Judging by the context and clarity of your letters to me, their confidence in you is well placed. I'm very proud of you and I'm delighted that we have become so close through our correspondence, even though we are separated by a large ocean and six or seven time zones.

Steve, I'm also sorry that our first telephone conversation was precipitated by such a horrible event, but I do have to say that I was thrilled to hear your voice for the first time. You sound just like I've always imagined your father sounded at your age. Sadly, I can only imagine, since I missed out on all of his formative teenage years – and all the years that have followed since we parted ways. I also hope and pray that he and I will talk again someday. When two worlds part because of differing ideologies, it's very difficult to bring them back together again – but not impossible!

Just a word or two about our present situation here in Israel. Ever since Arafat threw away a historic opportunity to forge a lasting peace with us (at Camp David in the summer of 2000), the PLO and other militant Palestinian organizations, like Hamas and Islamic Jihad, have been waging a war of terror against us in the insane belief that sending suicide bombers to target our civilian population will somehow help them to achieve their goal of destroying the State of Israel. In fact, they're destroying the hopes and aspirations of their *own people* who just want to live normal, prosperous lives in their own sovereign state of Palestine – side by side with Israel in a peaceful Middle East which we, and the rest of the civilized world, have prayed for, for so long. Terror, no matter its guise (Al-Qaeda, Hizballah, Hamas, etc.) will be defeated by the free peoples of this world.

That's enough talk about politics and war. Sareleh and I, and the rest of our family, are just fine. We're all looking forward to some warmer days now, as spring rounds the corner. Up here in the high country of the Upper Galilee, the winter chill sometimes lasts until the middle of May and snow remains on the peaks of

Mount Hermon until the latter part of June. It's really so beautiful. I hope someday you'll be able to enjoy our breathtaking view – in person.

In the meantime, please keep me posted about your upcoming trip to Colorado. I'm so excited for you – both about the Scout Ranch *and* your unexpected visit to the University of Colorado.

Sareleh sends her love along with mine,

Grandpa

May 8, 2002

Dear Grandpa,

Sorry for not answering your last letter sooner. I've been really busy studying for final exams and preparing for our last debate of this term. It's about a proposed reform to our Social Security law (old-age pension). It's a bit complicated, but as the law stands today, the Social Security funds may run out by the time I reach retirement age, or even sooner, if we don't change the way money is being invested now. Our team is taking the side for changing the law and I've been chosen by our coach to present the final arguments. I'm really excited about making my case! Maybe I should be a lawyer after all – ha ha!

I'm also starting to organize my clothes and camping equipment for this summer. I have this Tyrolean hiking hat that I've always worn on my camping trips, but I think I'm going to buy a Stetson cowboy hat for this trip. I'm not sure where they're sold here in the East, so I'll probably just wait until I get to Colorado to find one. I also thought I'd buy a pair of cowboy boots if we're going to be riding horseback.

Grandpa, I just want you to know that the Bowie camping knife you sent me for my bar mitzvah has been with me on *all* my camping trips since then, and it will be at my side on this trip to Colorado as well. Even though you never made it to the Ranch when you were a boy, you'll be there with me this time – in spirit! If you don't hear from me for the next month or so, don't worry. I'll just be really busy. I promise I'll write as soon as I get to the Ranch. Bye for now.

Love,

Steve

May 21, 2002

Dear Steve,

I will indeed be with you in spirit as you trek the mountain passes of America's mighty western highlands. Although I truly loved hiking in the older Appalachian range of America's east coast, I always had my eye and heart on those magnificent Rockies. I know you've probably seen hundreds of pictures of the Rocky Mountains, but if you want to enjoy a different visual and emotional experience, look up the photographer Ansel Adams on the Internet. His 1930s black-and-white stills of Yosemite National Park capture the very soul of Mother Nature's silent majesty. Better yet, maybe your local Barnes & Noble bookstore has a copy of his published photographs. They're a national treasure!

Steve, here I am rambling on about my own passions when all I really wanted to say was that I hope you have the time of your life. Take care of yourself. When you have a chance to jot down some notes in your journal, try and express what you're feeling at that very moment. Maybe someday you can publish your own book of "ramblings," as did Mark Twain about *his* adventures out west. His book is called *Roughing It*, if I remember correctly. Seriously, Steve, you do have a way with words and I'm looking forward to reading them. Have a safe and glorious journey. God's speed!

Love,

Grandpa

July 31, 2002

Dear Grandpa,

Just a quick postcard to tell you I had a fabulous week at the University of Colorado. Stayed in a fraternity house on campus. Took a Greyhound bus to Glenwood Springs. Bought myself a Stetson hat today and cowboy boots too. Truck from Ranch coming to pick me up in half an hour so got to go.

Thought you might enjoy this idyllic scene of tourists enjoying the splendor of the magnificent snow-capped peaks of the Rocky Mountains.

Love,

Steve

Courtesy: Glenwood Springs Chamber of Commerce

September 17, 2002

Dear Grandpa,

Sorry it's taken me so long to write, since I got home from my summer adventures out west. I've been really busy with the start of the school year. I'm a senior now and *all* my courses are really important. As you once suggested, I'm applying to lots of universities so that all my options will be open – hopefully!

So much has happened since I wrote you that postcard from Glenwood Springs that I really don't know where to begin. It all started out just as the brochure pictured it to be and, much to my surprise, it got even more exciting. It's a bit of a long story, so I'd better start from the beginning.

The Ranch is in the high country just outside the White River National Forest, which is one of the most beautiful in the whole country. It has thousands and thousands of acres of virgin forest and wilderness area, which was set aside by the government to be untouched for all time. Anyway, after a few days of orientation and preparation, about seven or eight of us older guys (seventeen- and eighteen-year-olds) set out backpacking up into the mountains with two experienced guides.

We first took a truck to a high base camp, which was on a ridge overlooking a spectacular gorge carved out by the Colorado River far below. On both sides of the canyon were rolling hills of forests as far as the eye could see. And on the horizon were the famous snow-capped Rocky Mountains, and here I was about to set out trekking on its high ridges with panoramic views that you only see in *National Geographic* magazine or, of course, Ansel Adams' beautiful black-and-white photographs of Yosemite National Park. By the way, before I left home, I looked him up on the Internet. There's something very special about that old-style black-and-white photography that color film just doesn't seem to have, so I brought along some black-and-white film to experiment with. I shot a couple of rolls, but I guess it takes a lot more experience with light and shades and shadows. They didn't turn out the way I'd hoped.

Anyway, back to my story! I forgot to tell you – I had a choice between a horseback trek or backpacking. I chose backpacking, of course, and I left my new cowboy boots behind, but I did wear that Stetson. It's a great hat! I'm enclosing a photograph of me and Pete. He's from Cincinnati, Ohio. I'm the guy on the left, if you can't recognize me with that ten-day beard. It itched like crazy, but I was determined to grow a beard, even if it was just for a few weeks.

Continuing on with my adventures, we were out on the trail for about four days when one of our guides got a call on his cell-phone from a ranger station about twenty miles from us. A small fire had been spotted in the general direction we were heading. It had been a very hot and dry summer and the rangers were advising all hikers and campers to evacuate the area. To our great disappointment, we were advised by the Scout Ranch officials to head for a specific road down from the ridge, where we would be picked up. And so (I thought) ended the summer's big adventure, backpacking in the high country of the beautiful Rocky Mountains.

Well, the backpacking trip did come to an abrupt end, but *not* the adventure. The best was yet to come! When we got back to the Ranch and had a good night's rest, we were told that a weeklong horseback trek had been arranged for us and that we would be heading out the following morning. We were supposed to be briefed and to get our provisions the next day. And just as an afterthought, the counselor in charge mentioned that the fire crews working this new fire could always use a hand or two at their base camp, helping out in the field kitchen and stuff. I jumped at the chance and convinced Pete to join me. I thought it would be a great experience, meeting those guys who actually go in and fight these fires face to face.

Anyway, the two of us were taken by truck about twenty miles down the main highway and then we turned off onto an old logging road which led up into the forest for another very bumpy few miles. By now we could actually feel the acrid smell of the forest fire in our nostrils, even though it was many miles away. When the dirt road finally began to level off, we found ourselves on top of a rocky ridge that looked out over thousands of acres of forest below. We could actually see the smoke from the fire, way off in the distance.

In the center of this treeless hilltop was a tall wooden tower with zigzaggedy stairs leading up to its watchtower. This was apparently the main ranger station in the area, now being used to coordinate all the firefighting crews working this latest summer fire. It was also the base camp and rest place for all the men (and women) fighting the fire. What I remember most about my first impression was the "blending" of smells. One was, of course, that horrible odor of the fire, which made my nostrils quiver. The second (and much more pleasant) was coming from over by the cooking tent. It was chili – Mexican style – and how I love chili! We were introduced to the cook and told to grab a mess kit (Boy Scout style) and help ourselves. There isn't anything better than fresh baked biscuits and chili and that was the best of both I ever tasted!

Basically, our job was to help the cook peel potatoes (lots of them), occasionally stir the pots of stew or whatever, wash all the pots and pans and mess kits and generally keep the whole cooking and eating area as clean as possible. In between, we got to meet all the firefighters. That's for another letter. Let me just say that I met a bunch of the best guys (and girls) you could ever want to meet. I finally found people like myself who would rather be out in the woods than anywhere else. Back home, I sort of feel different than all my school friends. In the mountains of Colorado, I really felt *at home*.

More next time.

Love,

Steve

P.S. Maybe I shouldn't say anything because I don't want to worry you, but you're my pen pal and I really don't have anyone else to talk to about it. Mom and Dad are going through one or their bad spells – they're arguing all the time. They try and hide it, but I hear them and it really bugs me. They usually make up in a few days, but this time it's longer. I hope they make up soon!

October 3, 2002

Dear Steve,

I was really excited to receive your letter about your extraordinary summer adventure out west. I must say you write beautifully. Your description of the White River National Forest sounded almost like poetry. Oh, how I wanted to go to the Scout ranch when I was your age! I guess fate had other plans for me, for which I am, now, eternally grateful. I fulfilled other dreams, and today I can even vicariously live those unfulfilled youthful dreams of mine through your wonderful letters.

Things are fine here on the kibbutz. Saraleh sends her love. We're putting the finishing touches to another 10 housing units and hopefully the families will be moving in before Hanukah. Since we began building almost four years ago, twenty new families have come to live with us here on our mountain. They're mostly young professional people who work in our growing hi-tech industries here in the Upper Galilee. Almost half the families are immigrants from the former Soviet Union who made aliyah as children in the early 90s, when the Iron Curtain finally came crashing down for good.

Even though the fifty-year "Cold War" between East and West is over, the world hasn't seen an end to oppressive tyrants. Now we've got Saddam Hussein to deal with. It looks like President Bush is going to have a hard time convincing the United Nations that Saddam's regime in Iraq is a real threat to the rest of the world. Even though the UN weapons inspectors haven't found them yet, it's a pretty sure bet that they do have a secret chemical, biological and nuclear weapons program. And Saddam has no qualms about using such weapons, either. He's already killed thousands with chemical weapons in Iran and used them against the Kurds in northern Iraq. I personally think the Americans should have taken him down in 1990/91 when they had a chance. As far as I can see now, the British are the only ones supporting the American position in the UN – and us, of course. Let's see what happens! In any case, our gas masks are being "updated" for any eventuality. Not to worry! We'll be well prepared for whatever comes our way. I only hope that if we are attacked, the Americans will let us hit back this time.

Getting back to your summer adventure, I have to tell you that I would have made the same decision – to go with the firefighters. No contest! We really are alike, you and I. Please tell me more about them in your next letter.

It's getting a bit late now, so I'm going to end with just a word about your postscript. Steve, please don't worry about your Mom and Dad. Couples have their periodic ups and downs. I'm sure everything will be fine. Just give them a little space until they've worked their problem through.

My very best to both your Mom and Dad.

Love,

Grandpa

October 18, 2002

Dear Steve,

Just remembered your eighteenth birthday is coming up on November 19th and I wanted to get this letter off early, so I won't miss the date. Eighteen... that's a big one. Mazal tov! I really do remember when I was eighteen and a senior in high school.. It seems like it was just yesterday, but in fact, this coming June will be the fiftieth anniversary of my high school graduation. I'll bet some alumni committee is probably planning a fifty-year class reunion. Our class had a lot of *esprit de corps* back then.

I can't believe a half-century has passed since those good old days at Weequahic High in Newark. I keep in touch with three of my high school buddies. Two of them still live in northern New Jersey and the third became a doctor in Holland. He married a Holocaust survivor. Sareleh and I went to visit them a few years ago, and they've come to Israel several times. His wife is involved in an Israeli women's organization. I still have my high school yearbook. All the kids wrote something under their pictures for posterity. I glance at it occasionally and wonder what all my classmates have done with their lives.

Our high school had quite a high national academic rating back then. Being totally honest, I'm a bit embarrassed to say that, unlike you, I wasn't on the high end of that "upward scholastic curve." In defense of her only son, my mother used to refer to me as a "late-bloomer," which was a kind way of explaining my under-achievement. After my army days, though, I did become a serious student, finally vindicating her unshakeable faith in my potential.

My mom was a great lady and I know you and she would have gotten along famously. My father was a good man, but when I was a teenager he was less sensitive to my unconventional outdoor-oriented lifestyle; He never quite understood who I was back then. I even liked country/western music before anyone else in New Jersey had even heard of it; Hank Williams, Hank Snow and Tennessee Ernie Ford were some of my favorite singers. Have you ever heard of them? I was also into serious folksingers like the legendary Woody Guthrie, who came to the fore during the Great Depression of the 1930s. Pete Seeger and Joan Baez followed in his footsteps, as well as Bob Dylan and Carole King a decade or so later.

Unlike his son's rather adventurous nature, my father's straight-laced, conventional life had been devoted to the clothing business. For him to have a son whose lifestyle was so different than his own must have been quite frustrating at times. Later in life, though, we sort of reached a plateau of understanding between us. We made our peace.

Anyway, I want to once again wish you a very happy birthday, and I hope your senior year in high school is the best ever.

My warmest regards to your folks.

Love,

Grandpa

December 3, 2002

Dear Grandpa,

Please forgive me for not answering your last letter sooner. I've been really busy with my studies. I'm taking the SAT next month.

Thanks so much for your birthday wishes. You're right! Eighteen is a special age. I guess it's more psychological than anything else, but I do feel "older." It's sort of a new stage in life, like when I turned thirteen and had my bar mitzvah. I guess you'd call it a "milestone." I also have another milestone to share with you, Grandpa. I did it! I broke one minute in the 100-meter butterfly. My personal best is now *0:59.03*.

I can vote now, too. I would have voted for Al Gore in the last election, but I'm not so sure he'd be the right president for us, now that we're at war. He was articulate and everything during the campaign (just like Clinton), but being the right man to wage an all-out war on terror is something else. Even though President Bush sometimes "mangles" the English language and acts more like a Texas cowboy than a president, I think he's the right man to lead us during these difficult times. My parents don't agree with me and we sometimes get into a heated debate over the present "state of the union." We usually end up agreeing to disagree.

Anyway, it looks pretty sure that President Bush is going to send our troops into Iraq to take down the Saddam Hussein regime – without waiting for UN approval. I think he's right! With

France, Germany and Russia against an invasion, there's no way it would ever pass a Security Council vote. We're going to have to go it alone (except for the British, that is). Blair's one of the good guys. It seems like he and Bush are standing together against the whole world. Is everyone blind to the potential danger of Saddam Hussein and his hidden weapons?

Enough of politics for now. I've got a feeling we're going to be hearing plenty about the Persian Gulf in the coming few months. It's my understanding that we have to go in pretty soon or the summer heat and sandstorms of the desert will delay the invasion till late fall – giving Saddam lots more time to prepare. Let's just do it already! The world will be a lot better off without the likes of Saddam Hussein and his henchmen.

Anyway, I never finished telling you about the great guys and gals I met last summer while I was working with the firefighters. There was a small group of them who are known as *smokejumpers*. They're the people who actually parachute into the heart of a forest fire in the hope of containing it before it has a chance to spread. I got really friendly with a couple of the guys and they told me a lot about their work. One of them, my new friend Dale, said smokejumpers are the "first line of defense." Nobody can respond to a wildfire in remote mountain terrain as quickly as they can. Simply put, these guys and gals put on jumpsuits, parachutes and old motorcycle helmets outfitted with metal grilles for facemasks and leap from planes to fight fires. Once on the ground, firefighting tools, food and water are parachuted in, making them self-sufficient for the first forty-eight hours.

I spent every spare minute I had talking with my new friends and learning about what they do. During the winter months, most of them have other jobs. My friend Dale works on a ranch where he lives with his family near his smokejumping base in Missoula, Montana. He said if I wanted a summer job on the ranch before starting school in the fall, he could arrange it for me. I'm really thinking seriously about his offer. I haven't mentioned it to Mom and Dad yet. Dale has become my second pen pal, except we e-mail each other. Grandpa, are you sure you don't want to get a computer? It's instant communication!

By the way, I never heard of those country/western singers you mentioned, but I certainly know about Woody Guthrie. Last year I did a book review of John Steinbeck's *Grapes of Wrath* and I came across his name during my background research. When I found out that he wrote: "*This Land is Your Land*" I bought all his CDs. He was not only a great folksinger and writer, but also an extraordinarily courageous man during a very sad time in American history. When he sings "*This Land*," I get goose bumps because I really know why he wrote it – it describes my feelings exactly. He was a great American patriot! The first verse of his great song goes like this. Do you remember it?

> *This land is your land, this land is my land,*
> *From California to the New York island;*
> *From the redwood forest to the Gulf Stream waters*
> *This land was made for you and me.*

That's all for now.
    Love,
        Steve

P.S. Happy Hanukah.

January 5, 2003

Dear Steve,
    Great going on breaking your one-minute barrier for the 100 meter butterfly. I'm so proud of you in so many ways!

Anyway, because of the holiday mail rush, I only received your last letter a few days ago. I must tell you that even though I haven't lived in America for many years, I was still moved when I read the words of Woody Guthrie's legendary song. They gave strength and a sense of belonging to many of that generation who felt lost and abandoned during a time of poverty, uncertainty and desperation in American history. I remember reading Steinbeck's *Grapes of Wrath* and coming away saddened and astonished that this could have happened in America – but it did!

An interesting side note: Did you know that the Broadway musical "Oklahoma" (written and scored by Rogers and Hammerstein) was a glorified version of the story of those very same optimistic pioneers who moved westward during the first decades of the twentieth century, and who settled and farmed the great central plains of the American mid-west? That lively musical, which debuted on Broadway in 1943 (during the most difficult days of World War II) was meant to cheer up a war-weary citizenry, rather than depicting the reality of what actually had happened to those naively optimistic new farmers. Their lack of experience and farming expertise, in such areas as proper methods of crop rotation and irrigation, brought about the devastating dustbowls and drought of the early 30s which, in turn, brought about the plight and wanderings of those desperate "Okies" in Steinbeck's novel. When *The Grapes of Wrath* was initially published in 1939, it was not very well received by the critics nor by the public. No one wanted to face the reality of that sad chapter in American history. However, Steinbeck's epic novel was eventually recognized as one of the finest works of American literature of the twentieth century and he was awarded the Pulitzer Prize for literature in 1940. But I'm sure you already knew that.

By the way, I'm a bit of a lyric buff myself. My favorite song from "Oklahoma" was called: "Oh what a beautiful morning" and it went something like this:

There's a bright golden haze on the meadow
There's a bright golden haze on the meadow
The corn is as high as an elephant's eye....
And it looks like it's climbing clear up to the sky...
Oh, what a beautiful morning, oh what a beautiful day,
I've got a beautiful feeling, everything's goin' my way
Oh, what a beautiful day!

I've known these great words and wonderful melody for well over fifty years, and you know what? Every now and then, I think of them and I just burst into song. It gives me a great feeling about life. I'm sure you understand what I mean.

And... with that note of optimism in the air, I've got some great news to share with you. As I mentioned, this coming June will be the fiftieth anniversary of my high school graduation, and as I suspected, there's going to be a reunion weekend held at the Marriott Hotel at Newark Airport. I've decided to make the trip. I'm trying to convince Saraleh to come with me, but she's a bit embarrassed about her English. I've told her it doesn't matter and that I'll translate anything she doesn't understand, but she's uncomfortable about spending an entire weekend in an English-speaking environment. I really do understand how she feels, but I'd still love her to come. I'll keep trying!

Anyway, it will be great fun to see all my old classmates again and catch up on what everyone has been up to these last fifty years. But best of all, you and I will have a chance to get together in person. I'll skip the sightseeing tours to our old high school and hangouts and you and I can spend the whole day together. I'll fill you in on the details as I know more. I'm really excited about my trip and spending time with you.

My best to your folks,
Love,
Grandpa

January 19, 2003

Dear Grandpa,

I'm so excited that you're coming to the States. How long will you be staying for? Maybe we can spend a few days together. I hope so! I hope Saraleh can come too. I'm really anxious to meet her. Please tell her that for me, will you? And tell her not to worry about the English – just come. Maybe she can teach me some basic Hebrew words and phrases. I've forgotten everything I learned for my bar mitzvah.

School ends on June 10th. Please write me all the details as soon as you can. Grandpa, we've been pen pals since I was twelve years old and this is the first time we're going to meet in person – I wish it could have been sooner.

Anyway, I took my SAT last week and I feel I did well. This year I'm really concentrating on my schoolwork. and doing all the paperwork to apply to several universities, as you suggested. However, my heart is set on a possible academic scholarship from the University of Colorado's School of Forestry. Along with my application, I sent them my C.V. with all my outdoor activities in the Scouts etc. – I even had Pappi write me a letter of recommendation. Signs are positive so far, but I won't get a final answer from them until March or April. By the way, I've made up my mind about this coming summer. My friend Dale arranged that summer job for me on the ranch up in Montana where he works during the winter months. If I'm accepted at Colorado it will work out great. I'll fly out to Montana after school ends, work for the summer on the ranch, and then start the fall semester at Boulder. I won't even have to fly back to New Jersey. I can have all my clothes and stuff shipped directly to the university.

That's why I need to know when you're coming and for how long. I'll adjust my schedule so at least we can have several days together – if that's possible from your side.

Grandpa, please write soon and let me know. I know it's only

January, but I'm already making my summer plans and I want to make sure I'm still here when you come. I'm so excited about spending time with you before I go out west.

Love,

Steve

P.S. I haven't mentioned your coming to Mom and Dad yet because I didn't know how you'd feel about that. Please let me know if I should tell them or not. I'll understand either way.

February 7, 2003

Dear Steve,

As usual, I was delighted to receive your last letter, especially this time, since it's a prelude to our very first meeting in person. Steve, I'm just as excited as you are about spending time together. I can't wait to see you "in the flesh" after all these years of writing letters back and forth across the ocean.

I do have some more information about our upcoming class reunion. It's going to be held at the Marriott Hotel at Newark Airport during the second weekend in June. I'll be flying in (by myself) on Friday, June 13th.

Unfortunately, Saraleh won't be making the trip with me, but it's not because of her hesitation about an all-English weekend. It's actually because a special event is taking precedence: our granddaughter Yael is being inducted into the army that very Sunday morning, and Saraleh doesn't want to miss seeing her off. I would have loved to be there too, but Saraleh convinced me that my class reunion and the opportunity it would give me to see you were not to be missed. Anyway, I'll have plenty of chances to visit Yael on her army base. It's only an hour's drive from our kibbutz. And she'll be home almost every weekend, as well. She wants to take the officers' course when she finishes basic training. We're so proud of her.

Now back to details of our reunion weekend. On Saturday, we're just going to hang out; catching up with one another's "adventures" of the last fifty years. (I'm the only one in our class who moved to Israel, so I'm anticipating quite a few provocative questions.) That evening, the reunion committee is planning a gala buffet dinner with nostalgic entertainment. It should be lots of fun. On Sunday they've arranged a field trip to our alma mater – Weequahic High and a pep-rally at the football stadium with cheerleaders of today's generation. They've even arranged a visit to some of our old hangouts like "Sid's Hotdog Haven". They say it's changed ownership several times, but apparently kept the same name. Besides their great hotdogs, they had the best *knishes* in all of Newark. Anyway, I'll gladly skip all that nostalgic stuff so you and I can spend all of Sunday together. On Monday an old buddy of mine has invited me to stay at his place on Lake Hopatcong. We've kept in touch over the years; mostly by letters but occasionally by phone when something dramatic happened, like the Yom Kippur War and, of course, 9/11. He was a photojournalist until his retirement several years ago. He's writing a book now about his travels around the world. On Tuesday afternoon, he'll drive me back to Newark Airport and I'll catch the midnight flight back to Israel.

Sunday the 15ᵗʰ will be our day together. I'm sorry I can't stay longer, but maybe our next visit will be here in Israel. In your first letter to me you wrote – and I quote, "P.P.S. Maybe someday I can come visit you?" I've saved that very first letter and all your letters since then. They're in an album entitled "Dear Grandpa." I hope that someday soon you'll be able to re-read your own letters to me from over the years. I cherish our correspondence and friendship, Steve, and even though your Dad and I seem to have irreconcilable differences (which is very sad) you have given my life a great joy and excitement as I've witnessed your "coming of age" through your letters.

Steve, I just know you're going to get that academic scholarship to the University of Colorado, and I'm delighted for you that it's in a field of endeavor that you have loved and enjoyed since your first introduction to the great outdoors. The Boy Scouts of America builds great men. I'm so proud of you, Steve. You can be sure I'll make another trip to the States for your graduation ceremony. That's a promise!

By the way, your plans for next summer sound great. Working on a ranch in Montana should be a lot of fun as well as a lot of hard work. I'm sure you'll meet some great people too. I'm already looking forward to your letters telling me about your experiences as a Montana cowboy.

All my love,
Grandpa

P.S. For now, I'd appreciate if you wouldn't mention anything to your folks about my trip to the States. I'll write them myself.

February 28, 2003

Dear Grandpa,

Well, we and the British are just about ready to strike at Saddam. It must be really hard for the troops to sit there in the heat of the Kuwaiti desert, just waiting for orders to attack. From what we see on TV though, they're highly motivated, well disciplined and anxious for orders to move out. The TV clips show them training in the desert with gas masks and all that protective clothing. I don't know how they can stand the heat. And the way those Marines yell and scream, I sure wouldn't want to be facing them in combat. Anyway, it should start any day now. Let's just do it already! – "It's time to rock 'n' roll, guys!"

That's what the hero of that hijacked plane said on 9/11 when they jumped the terrorists, bringing the hijacked plane down over the Pennsylvania countryside rather than letting it possibly attack the White House itself. When I think of what they did, I get all choked up. They were the real heroes of 9/11, together with all the police and firefighters who worked in the aftermath of the attack. I still can't understand how we let that terror attack happen to us. It reminds me of what I've read about Pearl Harbor. There must have been *some* indications of what the Japanese were up to. It's the same with these terrorists. The FBI or CIA should have picked up something. We should have been more prepared. Now, at least, they've created the Office of Homeland Security. I hope it works!

Grandpa, I'm *really* excited about your coming to the States. I'm sorry it can't be for longer, but you're right – next time, I'll make the trip to Israel, maybe for a couple of weeks over a summer break.

By the way, I think it's really nice that you saved all my letters. I saved yours too. They've meant a lot to me during these past years. I really felt bad when Dad stopped us from writing. But that's all over now, and you're coming soon. I'm really looking forward to *our Sunday in June*.

As you requested, I haven't mentioned anything to Mom and Dad, but I have to tell you something before you write to them. I know they're doing their best to hide it from me, but I can feel the tension between them. They've been having a hard time for a while now. It's upsetting, but as you suggested to me several months ago, I'm giving them a lot of space. I keep my life focused on my schoolwork and my friends. I'm only home to "sleep & eat," so to speak. Grandpa, I want to help them, but I don't know how. If I say anything, I'm afraid it'll make things worse by bringing everything out into the open. I think they're going to a marriage counselor, but I'm not sure. Now that you know the situation, you can write them (or not) as you think best.

It's strange; I thought I'd be a lot more upset about their problems than I am. I do feel badly that they're going through difficult times, but the truth is that I've been sort of "independent" from them for a long time. We're not some close-knit family. During my high school years, I've had my life – school, my friends and the outdoors – and they've had theirs. I love Mom and Dad, but our priorities are very, very different. I've felt this gap between us for a long time now, and I'm really okay with that. That's why I'm so much looking forward to leaving home and going out west to work and study. I don't mean to sound overly romantic about it, but I think my life was meant to be elsewhere. It wasn't by chance that I fell in love with the great outdoors. It was meant to be! It's more like your life, in a way. Destiny played a big part in your life. I think it's the same with me. We'll talk more about that when you get here – if that's okay with you. See you soon.

Love,

Steve

P.S. I had to ask Grandma what *knishes* are. They sound great only I think I'd like the potato ones rather than the kasha.

March 30, 2003

Dear Steve,

Well, we took our gas masks out of storage, updated them with new vials of atropine (an antidote to nerve gas), got our sealed rooms all fitted up with as many amenities as possible and waited for the first salvo of SCUD missiles to arrive from our nemesis, Mr. Saddam. We're still waiting… I don't think they'll be coming this time.

From what we've seen on TV, the American and British forces seem to be carrying the fight to the enemy, and it's predicted that within a week or so, the Americans will be in Baghdad and the Brits will occupy Basra in the south. Hope all goes as predicted. At least this time, they're going all the way. In the first Gulf War in 1990, President Bush (senior) halted the advance just when the U.S. forces could have wiped out Saddam's Republican Guard and brought down Saddam himself. I never understood that military misjudgment. I think it was Colin Powell's call. He was Chairman of the Joint Chiefs of Staff at the time. General Schwarzkopf, who was the commander in the field, went on record after the war as opposing the halt – an interesting point to be pondered by future military historians.

Anyway, we're all fine and – just like the rest of the world – we're tuned into CNN for the latest news. "Embedding" journalists with the troops is an interesting concept, but it seems to me that sitting in the back of a Humvee or other troop carrier doesn't give the war correspondents as much of a chance to feel the action around them as their predecessors had in previous wars.

I was only a little boy during World War II, but I remember that my father used to read us Ernie Pyle's column from our local evening paper – *The Newark Evening News*. Pyle wrote about his *feelings*, crawling under fire from foxhole to foxhole with the troops as they advanced, meter by meter, on some Japanese-held island in the South Pacific. It was so moving that I still recall the emotions we felt sitting around the kitchen table, listening to my father read aloud. Toward the end of the war, Ernie Pyle was killed by sniper fire on one of those remote Pacific islands.

Well, that's about all *my* feelings about the current war for now. I think I'll take some time out and compose a letter to your folks about my upcoming trip to the States. Of course, I won't mention anything about their "situation." I do hope they can work things out, but sometimes it's just not possible. Let's hope for the best for both of them.

I'll write soon again with an update on the war from our Middle East perspective.

Love,

Grandpa

April 5, 2003

Mr. & Mrs. Michael Friedman
1053 Claremont Road
Livingston, New Jersey 07039
U.S.A.

Dear Michael and Joan,

Just wanted to drop you a short note to let you know that my high school graduating class of June '53 is having a fiftieth-year reunion at the Marriott Hotel at Newark Airport on the weekend of June 14/15. I'll be flying in on the 13th and staying only for a few days. I've invited Steven to spend Sunday the 15th with me at the hotel. I hope that meets with your approval. He and I have become close pen pals over the years and I'm really looking forward to our first meeting in person. I'll call him as soon as I get in. He's a wonderful young man and I'm proud to be his grandpa.

Warm regards,
Dad

April 23, 2003

Dear Grandpa,

Mom and Dad are getting divorced. They told me last night before I went to bed. It was all very civilized and unemotional – too civilized, if you ask me. We had this talk and Mom did most of the talking. Dad just nodded and agreed with what she said, how their lives and interests have changed and grown apart over the years etc. etc.… and now that I'm older and going off to college etc. etc.… Mom will stay in the house for now and Dad will get a small apartment close to his work. Later, when the market is better, they'll sell the house etc. etc. Dad assured me that all my expenses for college

95

etc. have been put aside in a separate account and that I shouldn't worry about any financial matters.

Grandpa, I'm not worried about money, but I'm more worried about their breaking-up than I thought I'd be. I don't know why. We're not all that close and my life is so different and independent from theirs. But all the same, Grandpa, I'm very upset! I don't know why it's hit me so hard. I've known that they've had problems for years, but I never really thought it would lead to a divorce. They always seemed to work things out in the past. They didn't exactly say it in words, but I guess they tried to keep things together until I was ready to "leave the nest," so to speak. That's all well and good, but I still feel badly for them (and myself) even though I'm supposedly old enough to understand these things. The truth is that I really won't have a home to come home to any more. That reality makes me very, very sad.

Grandpa, I'm really looking forward to your coming to the States so we can talk in person. I wish you lived here! Anyway, another month and a half and we'll be together for our special day.

Lots of love,
    Steve

P.S. Mom and Dad got your letter and everything's okay. They told me you'd call me as soon as you get to the hotel.

See you soon,
    Steve

Part III

Meeting at the Marriott

Aside from one young couple checking-in, and the three attractive receptionists behind the elegant marble counter, the lobby of the Marriott Airport Hotel was virtually empty at seven o'clock on that particular Sunday morning in June. Not even a bellboy could be seen, until one emerged through the side entrance with the young couple's suitcases stacked neatly on the brass dolly he was pushing ahead of him. However, that special early morning tranquility could not be found in the large private dining hall on the mezzanine level at the far end of the main lobby.

A boisterous crowd of some 200 guests were enjoying an early breakfast before their departure on a day's adventure into the past – 50 years into the past to be exact. This was the fifty-year high school reunion of Weequahic High's class of '53 and they were in a joyful and gregarious mood as they ate and babbled about their youthful frivolities – all at the same time. Some of the alumni had brought their spouses, others came alone. But the curious thing was, that the same social cliques which had existed fifty years before, continued on throughout this reunion weekend. The, by now, barrel-bellied old "jocks" hung out together, reminiscing about old glories on the grid-iron and the basketball court, which, at the time, had defined their status among the student body at this prestigious secondary school in the heart of Newark's Jewish neighborhood. The honor-students as well also seemed to congregate together, comparing notes about their achievements in industry and the academic world.

Yoram/Richie (as he was known back then) Friedman was in neither of these two major social categories. He had been an average student, just keeping his grades high enough to placate his parents and to ensure that he would be allowed to continue his scouting activities and go on his next camping trip into the great outdoors. This was his life and his passion; although a girlfriend or two snuck in occasionally to capture his heart.

He did have a few close buddies during those wondrous high school years and miraculously the "four musketeers", as they called themselves, had managed to keep in touch over the years. Ronnie, Woody and Barry had come with their wives. Yoram had flown in alone but armed with an entire photo album of his Israeli family and an exuberant explanation of his granddaughter's induction – that very weekend – into the Israel Defense Forces. And of course, there were endless stories about his adventurous American grandson Steve, whom they would actually be meeting on Sunday.

It was eight o'clock now and four chartered buses were waiting for the Weequahic High School alumni to take them on a nostalgic trip to their almamater as well as a peek at some of their old teenage haunts. The reunion weekend would culminate with a mid-afternoon picnic in Weequahic Park – near the lake; a beautiful spot, and for some, a lovely memory of their very first romantic encounter on the grassy slopes leading to its gentle shoreline.

Richie walked his friends out to the buses. He wouldn't be taking this trip down memory lane with his old classmates. He had other plans for that special Sunday. His grandson Steve would be coming to the hotel within the hour for their first face-to-face meeting – after many letters between them had crisscrossed the Atlantic Ocean during the last six years.

It was close to nine o'clock when a rather tall lanky young man came through the revolving doors of the Marriott's front entrance. Yoram was sitting in a lounge chair, with an unobstructed view of those revolving doors. When he recognized his grandson coming at him with the stride of an Olympic runner, he was a bit taken aback by Steve's unexpected height.

"*He must be at least six feet tall!*" he thought to himself. Yoram himself was only 5'9" and his son Michael was not that much taller.

"*It must be 'Wheaties' – The Breakfast of Champions*", he thought to himself in a millisecond of private humor. And then in another moment of pure joy, he jumped into the outstretched arms of his beloved pen pal. Both men were unashamedly crying.

During that special Sunday, both grandfather and grandson would confide in one another more than either could have anticipated. Yoram was more like an older friend and confidant to Steve, rather than a grandpa in the traditional sense of the role. He was that idealistic "dreamer" and "Boy Scout" who had chosen a different path in life – and paid a heavy price for following his dreams. Steve admired him more than anyone he had ever known. And on the other side of the coin, in Yoram's heart, Steve had become the son incarnate; the son who would not have deserted him so many years ago. In the privacy of Yoram's room, it was so easy... and natural, for both men to "open up" and bare their souls to one another. Both had a great need to do so. Steve went first. His need was the greater... and more immediate!

"Grandpa, I don't know why it's hit me so hard. I know I shouldn't be... but I'm angry at them. Here I am, just about ready to start my life... and they throw me this "curve-ball". What do they think... I don't have any feelings; that their splitting up wouldn't affect me?". Yoram just listened as his grandson continued – almost non-stop; his surprisingly deep voice vibrating with the emotions of a much younger version of himself. Steve was hurting deeply and his grandfather was the only person in the world to whom he would allow himself to burst open and let it all come out.

"I guess I sort of knew it was coming for a long time, but I didn't want to think about it. I'm really independent from them – for a long time now. I can take care of myself. It's not that. I guess it's the thought of not having a real home to come home to anymore... no matter if it wasn't the best of homes like some of my friends have. But still... it was *my* home! Do you understand, Grandpa?"

"Of course I do, Steve."

"And the thing is Grandpa, after I leave home this summer, I can never really go home again. And that makes me very, very sad... and angry too! Why did they have to do this now? I was so excited about going to the university in the fall... and now, I just don't know. I'm just not in the mood to be a serious student right now – even in forestry. It's too many changes all at once. I thought I could handle everything. I was ready to take on my whole future and I was really excited. But now, I'm not sure about anything anymore". And Steve began to cry. He had never allowed himself to cry in front of his parents, but with his grandpa... that was different.

"Steve, what you're feeling now is probably... no *absolutely* the most natural reaction to what's happening in your life right now. And what's more, if you weren't feeling this way, I'd be a bit surprised and more than a bit concerned that you were bottling everything up inside – and that's not healthy. You're doing just fine, Steve". Yoram held his grandson in his arms.

"Grandpa, I've always had this sort of "base camp" where I could come back to after school or my camping trips or after... after anything, and I always had my room, Mom and Dad, my friends. Now everything's going to be different like... like Dad always gave me his cell-phone and an extra battery whenever I went out on one of my outdoor adventures – just in case of an emergency. I never really had to use it, but now, who am I going to call if I need help or something? Mom and Dad have enough problems of their own. I wouldn't bother either of them! I don't really have anybody else except you, Grandpa – and you live all the way over in Israel!"

Yoram measured his words very carefully. Rarely was he called upon to exhibit such self-control as he demanded of himself at that moment. Steve was hurting badly and his anger at his parents was certainly understandable. Yoram was also angry at his son and daughter-in-law for many of his own reasons. But all those "old wounds" had to be put aside as he tried to comfort his grandson at this difficult juncture in the boy's life.

"Steve, please listen to me. First of all, your Mom and Dad will always be there for you", he said, not really whole heartedly believing this to be true. But he had to say it anyway.

"Steve, don't leave them out of your life because you think you'll be bothering them. Remember, if you make them feel like you're deserting them because of their problems, that will make them feel even worse than they already do". Yoram took a few moments to try and think of what to say next. It finally came to him.

"I know this whole business has shaken you up, but you can't let it really get to you. You're strong and self-reliant. I know you Steve. Your letters told me who you are. I love you as my grandson, but just as strongly, I respect you as a man. All those years in the Scouts you learned survival skills; the ability to make the best of any situation. Well, it doesn't just apply to the great outdoors. It's about life and how to survive its ups and downs. I know you, Steve, and I know you have what it takes to survive – and thrive. Even though you're hurting right now, I know you can begin this new chapter in your life... on your own. You're your own best support. Believe it!" And with that positive declaration, Yoram decided it was time to stop talking and give his grandson some "breathing-room". It was a good decision.

After a few moments of silence, Steve began to speak. This time, however, his voice was somewhat calmer... and more focused.

"Grandpa, I've actually made a decision that I haven't told Mom and Dad about yet. I'm not really sure if I'll tell them right now... or not! I've decided to take a year off and just work on the ranch. Dale set it up for me. I'm flying out to Montana next week. I also spoke to the dean of the Forestry School and I asked him if it would be possible to keep my scholarship until next year. I explained my situation to him and he was really understanding. I mean I really told him about Mom and Dad and everything, and that I decided to work on the ranch for a year. I even gave him Dale's cell-phone number as a reference. He said that that wasn't necessary but to keep in touch with him during the year... and that my scholarship would be waiting for me. But anyway, Grandpa, that's what I've decided to do. Whatd'ya think?"...

...Yoram hesitated a tiny bit longer than Steve would have liked, but when he finally spoke, he came out with a strong and clear message to his grandson.

"Steve, I knew you'd know what to do! Your decision is the right one... and more importantly, you've got great instincts. You know yourself and you decide things accordingly – *Kol Hakavod!*" Steve looked at Yoram inquisitively.

"What Grandpa?"

"Oh sorry... that's Hebrew for – *all my respect!*"

"Thanks Grandpa!" By this time, both men were hungry and decided to adjourn for lunch. It had been quite an emotional morning for both of them.

During that special Sunday, Yoram and Steve closed the generation gap. There's no other way to put it. Although chronologically separated by more than half a century, these two people behaved as two close friends – buddies! Their dialogue, their body language and gestures... and their bonding was that of two equals – contemporaries if you will. So much so, that Yoram also was able to let himself go (so to speak) and confide in his new "best friend" about his own deep sorrow and greatest loss; the love and affection, and respect, of his only son, Steve's father – Michael.

Strangely, or maybe not, the fissure which eventually caused the breakup of Yoram's little family was based, for the most part, on a political ideology – Zionism. Ever since his youthful days as an American soldier in occupied Germany in the early '50s, Yoram had dreamed of someday moving to the newly created State of Israel. Post-war Germany still reeked with the smoke and ashes of the Holocaust – a powerful stench which would have a profound effect on the young Jewish American soldier. Less than two decades later,

Yoram would take his wife and young son from the relative "good life" in America to the uncertainties of an adventurous pioneering life in Israel. Steve listened intently and with great empathy as Yoram retold him the story of the Yom Kippur War and its personal aftermath upon his family. This time though, the emphasis was on his utter devastation when Steve's father rejected his Zionist values and willingly returned to America with his mother.

"The worst thing was..." Yoram explained with a cracking, emotional voice, "...is that your father believed – even to this day – that I deserted him by not returning to the States. I guess he thought I didn't love him enough to follow him back to America. I loved him very much... and I still do." And with that emotional outpouring of his unrequited love for his only son, he burst into tears. Steve knelt down beside Yoram's chair and held his grandfather in his arms. They both wept. Steve's only words were:

"I'm so sorry, Grandpa."

It was a little after seven o'clock in the evening when the buses returned to the hotel. Yoram and Steve were waiting in the lobby. Yoram wanted to introduce his grandson to the other "musketeers" before Steve had to drive home. His father had lent him that big Toyota Land Cruiser for the day... but it was getting late. When Ronnie, Woody and Barry and their wives spilled through those revolving doors, the two Friedmans were there to greet them. After the usual questions about his future, and the amazed and admiring adjectives they bestowed upon him about his unusual responses, Steve nodded to Yoram that he better get started home. It would be better to be a little early... than a little late. Yoram walked him out to the parking lot.

As they approached the car, Yoram decided to make a last-minute pitch to Steve about something he had been contemplating all day long but which, for whatever reason, had not quite gotten around to asking his grandson. Yoram tried to sound matter-of-fact, but in reality, his heart was racing with anticipation.

"Steve, what do you think about coming to visit us in Israel over the Christmas vacation?" Before Steve had a chance to respond Yoram continued in quick succession.

"We'll take care of your round-trip ticket and everything. We'll pick you up at the airport and you'll be with us – with your Israeli family – for all of Hanukah. And don't forget – Saraleh's a great cook!" he concluded as an added incentive. It wasn't necessary.

Steve's reaction was so lightning-fast that it took Yoram by complete surprise – in the most wonderful way.

"You know what, Grandpa? That sounds like a great idea. I'd love to come! I'm sure I get a Christmas vacation at the ranch. But just one thing," he added proudly, "I'll be working now, so I'm going to pay for half the fare. Okay?"

"Okay!" Yoram sputtered out. "What a wonderful thing to look forward to. It's only six months away! Saraleh and the whole family will be thrilled. I can't wait to tell them."

"I'm really excited too, Grandpa."

"Write me as soon as you get to the ranch, okay?" Yoram said as Steve turned on the ignition.

"I will, Grandpa! Have a safe trip home... and give my love to Saraleh .

"I will... bye. I love you!"

"Love you too, Grandpa... bye!"

*   *   *

June 29, 2003

Dear Grandpa,

Hi from Montana! It's Sunday morning here and this is the first chance I've had to write you since I got here last Wednesday. As you can see, I'm back to writing in longhand. I didn't even bring my laptop with me. It just doesn't fit out here with what I'm doing.

Grandpa, I have something to confide in you. I apologize in advance for not having shared this secret sooner. As close as we've become over the years, I didn't have the courage to tell you *every-thing* about what I'll be doing out here in Montana. I simply thought you might want to talk me out of it, and that would have ruined our one special day together.

As I told you at the hotel, I'll be working on a ranch with my friend Dale, but that's only starting in October. Right now I'm begin-ning my training as a firefighter and smokejumper. I've wanted to do this ever since I saw their work last summer. I hope you're not too shocked and I do apologize for not confiding in you about this, but I hope you understand why I didn't tell you during the one day we had together. I didn't want anything to spoil it for either of us. Please forgive me! I do plan on writing Mom and Dad about my decision to get a year's "field experience" working for the Montana forest service before I begin my university studies. However, I'm not going to mention the smokejumping, since I don't think they could handle that right now. I don't want to cause them any more trouble or anxieties than they already seem to have.

Anyway, now on to a short recap of my travels and new adven-tures. I left Newark Airport early Wednesday morning and, after a four hour flight, we landed in Butte. From there, I took a small twin-engine Cessna (with a few other passengers) to Missoula, Montana. Grandpa, we flew over some of the most beautiful wil-derness country I've ever seen. We were flying pretty low (about 3,000 feet) so this time, my view of the Rocky Mountains was "up close and personal." It was a magnificent hour's flight, which I'll never forget. To top it off, my friend Dale was actually waiting for me on the tarmac when we landed. The pilot's a friend of his and radioed ahead. It was so great seeing him again after a whole year! We've been corresponding by e-mail since last summer in Colorado.

Anyway, after we got my two duffle bags off the plane, we drove his vintage Willys jeep (the original 4×4) over to the far end of the airport where the smokejumper base is located. I must admit that my first impression of the base was a bit disappointing. I didn't really know what to expect, but at first glance it seemed a bit sparse for such an important part of the forestry service. As we approached, all I could see were three small planes sitting off to one side of the main runway, a couple of old battered-up 4×4s and two corrugated metal Quonset huts; the same kind they show in old World War II movies, only these were painted fire engine red, rather than the camouflage of yesteryear.

What made it seem even further from my romantic preconception of a smokejumper base was that no one seemed to be around. It just looked like some deserted corner of the main airfield. I guess I had imagined it to be more like an army training camp – only civilian. When I blurted out my surprise that no one seemed to be around, Dale explained that everyone was out at the actual training camp a few miles from the airfield. We were at the base headquarters and command center, equipment storage, eating and sleeping facilities and, of course, the airstrip.

The "everyone" he was speaking about consisted of two parachute instructors, ten experienced smokejumpers taking a refresher course, and three new recruits. I was the fourth recruit and at eighteen-and-a-half, the youngest they had ever accepted for the course. I felt very special – and privileged. Dale is the assistant base manager, and he must have said some pretty nice things about me to get me accepted. He's a great guy!

Anyway, we went into one of the huts to meet the boss, base manager John Warnecker, better known as "Warny." He seems to be a pretty nice, fiftyish guy. He's got a crew cut like a Marine drill sergeant but he's soft spoken and welcomed me warmly. His "office" (if you could call it that) consists of a makeshift desk (an old door) sitting on top of two wooden "horses" with lots of helter-skelter paperwork, two telephones, and a Motorola walkie-talkie. The wall behind him is "decorated" with aerial maps of the entire western United States... and then there are all these short-wave radios emitting a background hissing sound, occasionally silenced by the quacking of a human voice. Apparently the transmissions weren't for us, since Warny and Dale ignored them and just kept on talking about something or other. When they were finished, Warny shook my hand and wished me good luck in the course. It was a really nice welcome.

We each slung a duffle bag onto a shoulder and made our way over to the other hut, which is the army-style living quarters for all single personnel – that's me! I was really anxious to get out to the training site, so we just threw my gear on an empty bunk, hopped in the jeep and took off. It was only a five-minute ride, but when we got there, I said to myself, *"Now this is more like it!"* It wasn't exactly an army paratrooper base, but it did have a jump tower and an obstacle course. I thought I could handle the obstacle course pretty easily, but I wasn't so sure about that jump tower. It looked pretty imposing! I knew I'd have to come to terms with it.

Dale introduced me to everyone: instructors, veterans and the three other new recruits – two guys and a girl, all in their early twenties. I found out later that Janet is twenty-three and a school-teacher during the rest of the year. She really caught my eye... but I'm only eighteen! Oh well, there's no harm in dreaming.

Anyway, for the next couple of days, I got myself settled in and started my mandatory physical training to show that I was in good enough shape to take the course. First a doctor gave me a pretty thorough physical exam including an EKG. I passed with flying colors. Then there were all those push-ups and sit-ups and pull-ups and running the obstacle course (more than once), which was actually a lot of fun. But then came the cross-country running. That's hard! Three miles in less than half an hour. I did it! I quali-fied and tomorrow I start the real training to be a firefighter and smokejumper – which includes three hours of classroom work a day. This is serious stuff!

That's all for now, Grandpa. Dale's picking me up soon for lunch out at the ranch. It's only about twenty miles from here. He lives there all year long with his wife Sally Jo and their ten-year-old daughter Tammy. They have a trailer house. I'm really anxious to see the ranch. That's where I'll be working, starting in the fall.

Love to you and Sareleh and my whole Israeli family,
Steve

P.S. Would you believe I'm actually getting paid while I take this course? Not much, but it's my first real job! And the best thing is, it's going to pay for my ticket to visit you. I can't wait!

July 18, 2003

Dear Steve,

It's taken me a while to catch my breath after receiving your last letter – and even longer yet, to organize my thoughts in order to pen them to you now.

First of all, I want to assure you that I do understand and appreciate your motivation in not telling me "everything" during the one day we had together last month. With the multitude of emotions we expressed and shared that day, I agree that the inherent controversy of what you have just revealed to me would have definitely distracted both of us from "letting our hair down" and enjoying our wonderful day.

However, having said all that, I must confess that it is indeed quite a shock for me to learn about the true nature of your summer job – firefighting and smokejumping. And as you pointed out, this is your very *first* job! That's quite a "leap" into adulthood, if you'll forgive the pun. Seriously though, I am honestly overwhelmed with conflicting reactions, which are a bit complicated to explain, but I'll try. Please bear with me.

Having lived more than half my life here in Israel, I have embraced with all my heart the cultural mores, habits, ethics, emotions, patriotism and even the often-misunderstood "bravado" of my fellow countrymen. I am a proud Israeli patriot!

Now, I'm sure that at this point you're wondering to yourself, *"What in the world has all that got to do with my becoming a smoke-jumper?"* Well, it influences the way in which I perceive your dramatic disclosure. Do I see it with the eyes and mind-set of an Israeli grandpa, or, on the other hand, from the viewpoint of my former self of almost a lifetime ago – that of a typical American Jewish father? These are two very different reactions to the same stimuli. I know all this sounds a bit esoteric, but hang in there, I promise I'll bring it all together – eventually!

Let's start with the most likely reaction of a typical American Jewish father – or mother, for that matter. Here's how the conversation goes:

"What? My son's going to jump out of an airplane into the middle of a forest fire? Is he crazy? What kind of boy did we raise – an idiot? Look at Sara and Sam's boy… he's already in law school! And what about Hanna and Max's boy… what's his name… oh yes, Sheldon. He's going to be an architect. And our boy's going to jump out of airplanes for a living? What did we do wrong, George?"

Of course I'm exaggerating in order to make that stereotype conversation humorous, but the bottom line is very clear – NICE JEWISH BOYS DON'T JUMP OUT OF AIRPLANES!

Now for the reaction of a typical Israeli mother, father, grandma, grandpa, sister, brother, aunt, uncle or family friend: "Did you know that our Yigal just finished the paratrooper course? We were at the ceremony when he got his wings. We're so proud of him! Here, let me show you the photographs."

Steve, I'm sure that by now, you realize where I'm coming from. Even though I'm *mostly* an Israeli grandpa, there's still a tiny bit of "Jewish American father" left in my psyche. Please take care of yourself! I'm very proud of you. Write again as soon as you can. I want to hear all about your training.

Love,

Grandpa

August 5, 2003

Dear Grandpa,

I really had a good private laugh when I read your last letter. You've got to be Jewish to appreciate the humor. And out here in Montana, there's not a Jewish family to be found within a hundred-mile radius of Missoula, probably more, so I can't share it with anyone except you.

I do understand what you were trying to express with that "old-fashioned" conversation of the Jewish American parents, but I don't think it's as true today as it may have been a generation or so ago – at least I hope not! Anyway, with so many Jews intermarrying, it's hard to conceive of a Jewish stereotype these days – except for maybe those religious Jews in Brooklyn. I am also well aware (and proud) of my Israeli counterparts who are called upon, at my age, to put their lives on the line in defense of their country. In my opinion, their "bravado", as you put it, has been well earned.

I've been asked by my new friends about being Jewish, because the name Friedman is obviously Jewish, but no one seems to make a big deal of it. It's mostly just curiosity – some of them have never met a Jew before – and then they forget about it. Anyway, my being Jewish just isn't a factor out here. As a matter of fact, I've been given my own "handle," or nickname. They call me "Jersey." I like it! The instructors, though, call me "Hey, kid!" which is okay too – at least for now. After I make my first jump (which is next week), I'm sure they'll call me "Jersey", just like the others.

Grandpa, I've got so much to tell you, I don't know where to start. Oh, by the way, I called both Mom and Dad and told them I had decided to work on the ranch for the year before beginning school. They seemed to accept my decision without much comment. I guess they're both preoccupied with adjusting to their separate lives. Anyway, they seem fine and both assured me that they have

112

complete faith in my judgment and if I needed anything, not to hesitate to call. I'm sure they were sincere. I know they love me, but I'm glad I don't need anything. I don't want to bother them. I just want them both to be happy.

Now back to my adventures during these past weeks of training. First of all, I've made some great new friends. The veterans are all in their thirties and forties. Some of them who have families live off base, of course. The others bunk in the Quonset hut, like me. The two women veterans and Janet live in a motel just down the road. I'm still hung up on Janet, but I'm too embarrassed to even talk to her alone. Still just dreaming.

Anyway, our training is really intense. We're up at five o'clock in the morning for a two-mile run, after which we come back to a great breakfast – steak, bacon/ham and eggs, pancakes – anything you want – with great coffee to wash it all down. Then we're off to that training base I wrote you about.

By the way, I should explain that, while we four new recruits are training, Dale and the other veterans have already jumped six wildfires this summer. One of them was again down in Colorado in the White River National Forest. Probably careless campers!

Anyway, back to our training. We've been practicing (on the ground) how to exit an aircraft from about 3,000 feet, and steer our way down into the middle of a fire zone. The emphasis is on *steering*, so we can avoid (if possible) landing in the trees. But if we do get hung up in a tree, we've been taught how to get ourselves down with a "letdown rope." It's pretty tricky, but I've gotten the hang of it. We also practice landing rolls and jumping (with safety straps) from that imposing jump tower I mentioned in my last letter. I finally came to terms with my fear and just did it. Another basic part of our training is learning how to pack our chutes, which we do at least once a day.

Since, first and foremost, smokejumpers are firefighters, our class-room work has focused on methods of containing and extinguishing wildfires in remote areas that are inaccessible by other means. We also learn and practice first aid since we are pretty well isolated out there for the first twenty-four to forty-eight hours. Food and supplies are dropped to us by parachute. When we're all suited up and ready to go, we look a bit like men from outer space. We don jumpsuits and heavy-duty work boots, then strap parachutes on our backs, reserve chutes to our chests, and gear bags around our waists. Then we top off our outfits with old motorcycle helmets fitted with metal grill face masks… completing the picture of "creatures from the planet Mars."

As I mentioned, next Monday morning the four of us will be making our first jump. I'm both excited and scared at the same time. We'll be jumping from a twin prop DC-3 at about 3,000 feet. The first jump won't be close to trees. That comes next! I feel I'm ready and so do my instructors, so wish me luck! By the time you receive this letter, I'll probably have made four or five more jumps. The four of us won't be jumping wildfires this season – only next summer – if we all qualify.

That's about it for now. Hope all is quiet in Israel. I see those horrible terror attacks on television and I can't help worrying about you and Saraleh. When will it all stop?

Love you, Grandpa,

Steve

P.S. I've mentioned to some of my close friends out here that my grandfather lives in Israel. Their unanimous comments about Israel and Israelis was admiration. Since they're all Christians of one denomination or another, their reaction both surprised and pleased me. I had no idea that out here in the Rockies people actually had an opinion about Israel and the Middle East – except for Iraq, of course.

* * *

After Steve made that first adrenaline charged jump, there was no way he was just going to write a letter about it. This was an occasion for a surprise phone call to his beloved pen pal.

"Hello?"

"Hi, Grandpa, is that you?"

"Steve… hi! Is everything all right?"

"Everything's great, Grandpa! I made my first jump today, and it was fantastic! I didn't want to wait to tell you in a letter. I had to call and tell you in person!"

"Mazal tov! That's great, Steve. *Kol Hakavod!*"

"The four of us jumped early this morning and we all landed within twenty yards or so of each other. It was great! After breakfast we went up again for a second jump. It was… It was great! We're all still, like, on this high!"

"It sounds like it! I can hear it in your voice. I'm so glad you called, Steve. I've been wondering how your training was coming along… and of course, about how your first jump would go."

"I wrote you a letter about our training a few days ago, but you probably won't get it for another week or so. When we jumped today, I just had to call and share it with you right away."

"Steve, I'm so glad you did. I'm really proud of you!"

"Thanks, Grandpa. How are Sareleh and the rest of the family?"

"Everybody's just fine, Steve. Saraleh's visiting a friend in Haifa, but I'm going to call her right away and share your news with her, too. She'll be really happy you called!"

"Send her my love, Grandpa. I'll write again soon. Actually, I'm calling from the base telephone, so I'd better keep it short. Everybody here knows about you and they all wanted me to call. They all say 'Hi from Missoula, Montana.'"

"Say hi to everybody for me, too. Take care of yourself, Steve, and write soon, okay?"

"I will, Grandpa. Love you!"

"Love you, too. Bye!"

"Bye."

© Copyright Palphot Ltd., Herzlia, Israel.

August 15, 2003

Picture Postcard from Israel
    to
Steve Friedman and Friends
Missoula Smokejumper Base
Missoula International Airport
Missoula, Montana
U.S.A.

Dear Steve et al,
    Enjoyed your phone call so very much! Saraleh and I feel that

what you're all doing is both immensely important for the preservation of America's natural wilderness areas and (to say the least) a most courageous endeavor. *Kol Hakavod* (all our respect!).

Thought you might enjoy this view of the Jordan River, with Mount Hermon on the horizon.

Best wishes,

Saraleh & Yoram Friedman,
Kibbutz Misgav-Am, Israel.

September 5, 2003

Dear Grandpa,

Great news – we all graduated! The four of us have completed the course and we are now officially smokejumpers. I'm so excited! I'm not even nineteen yet and I've actually qualified for one of the most specialized jobs in the U.S. Forestry Service. There was even a special ceremony for us. It was really nice.

But before I get into all that, I wanted to thank you for sending that beautiful postcard to all of us here at the base. Everyone was really amazed that Israel has such beautiful mountainous terrain – just like Montana. Thanks again, Grandpa!

Now on to the continuation of my adventures. Since my last letter, we've made ten more jumps, each time honing our skills at steering as we descend. Even though I've gotten pretty good at it, I did get hung up in a tree one time. I got a bit bruised, but nothing serious. I let myself down with a rope (just as we were taught) and went on with our assigned work. Actually, the four of us have become really close these last two months. We've gone through some pretty hard training together. And since that first jump, the instructors do call me "Jersey".

As a matter of fact, a lot of things have changed since that first jump, especially something truly extraordinary that has literally changed my life. It's very personal and I wouldn't share it with anyone except you. I finally got up the courage to talk to Janet (one-on-one) and it seems that, even though there's a difference in our ages, she's also attracted to me. During the summer, other guys tried to get close to her, but she always managed to adroitly sidestep their amorous advances while, at the same time, maintaining their comradeship. That says a lot about her! We all thought that she probably had a serious boyfriend back home, but since she never mentioned him, I finally decided to take a chance and go for it.

I think I mentioned in my previous letters that I had been pining over her ever since I got here. Anyway, one day after work we just started talking, and to my utter amazement, we kept on talking well into the night – ending with a kiss that I could never have imagined before it actually happened. That evening we both felt we had found a soul mate in each other; a feeling I've only shared with one other person in my life – and that's you, Grandpa. I had a few girlfriends in high school, and each one was very special at the time, but I've never felt like I feel when I'm with Janet. And the most wonderful thing of all is that she feels the same way about me. When we're together, we don't notice the difference in our ages. We're just two people who love sharing a part of ourselves with each other. It's the most beautiful thing I have ever experienced in my whole life.

Realistically though, Janet and I both know that when she goes back home to her teaching job next week, it's likely we'll never see each other again. Next summer she'll be working at the Winthrop base up in the Cascades of Washington State. I'll be stationed here in Montana next summer and, after that, I'm starting forestry school at the University of Colorado. Our summer romance has been one of the most beautiful things that has ever happened to me, but Janet and I both know we have different journeys to travel in life and we've decided just – to remember. Like Barbra Streisand's sentimental ballad "The Way We Were" – it will be a beautiful memory. I know it sounds corny, but I feel privileged that this wonderful new experience was with Janet. I'll never forget her!

Forgive me, but I'm feeling a bit sad now because we'll be separated soon. I'll end this letter by saying how grateful I am that I'm able to share my most intimate feelings with you, Grandpa. You are my best friend!

Love,

Steve

P.S. I'll be here at the base till the middle of October, since we have a lot of equipment to clean and store. Afterwards, I'll be at the ranch.

P.P.S. I'm not exactly sure when the High Holidays come this year, since there aren't any synagogues out here in the mountain country, but I want to wish you and Saraleh and the whole family a Shana Tova! I'm really looking forward to visiting you in Israel over the Christmas/Hanukah vacation. I can't wait to meet my whole Israeli family. See you soon!

* * *

It was just ten days after Steve had posted this last letter to Yoram, that an extraordinary phone call came into the office at the smokejump base.

"Yeah…" Warny answered in his usual gruff manner.

"Ah… hello… Is this the smokejumpers?" Saraleh asked in hesitant and labored English.

"Yes… Who is this speaking?" Warny said more politely, taken aback by the foreign-accented voice on the other end of the line.

"I'm calling from Israel to speak to Steven Friedman, please. Is he there?"

"Yes!… just a moment, ma'am, I'll get him. Please hang on!" Warny said a bit forcefully, realizing from the sound of Saraleh's quavering voice that something was not right. Swinging his swivel chair around, Warny hit the intercom button behind his desk and shouted, "Jersey! Are you there?"

"Yeah, I'm here, Warny. What's up?"

"C'mon over! You've got a phone call."

"I'll be right there!" Steve shouted back, realizing that a phone call directly to the base meant something was wrong. No one except Yoram and Saraleh knew he was here, not even his parents. His father had called once to the ranch and they had used a pre-arranged cover story. Steve called his father back within a few hours. It was just one of those "parent" things. He had forgotten to call that week and touch base with his folks, as he had promised to do. This time all sorts of other possibilities went through his mind. Janet wouldn't call. They had decided to end their romance without lingering sentiment – just lovely memories. Anyway, if it were Janet on the phone, Warny would definitely have made some cute remark, since everyone knew, of course.

"So who could it be? Maybe it's Grandpa. Maybe he and Saraleh are planning a trip to the States and they can visit me out here in Montana. That would be fantastic!" he was saying to himself as he entered the office and took the phone from Warny.

"It's from Israel!" Warny said, with an odd sort of look.

"Hello..." Steve said anxiously, almost certain that it was Yoram on the other end of the line.

"Hello, Steve, this is Saraleh."

Within a millisecond, Steve's heart was beating as fast as if he were about to leap from a plane. Something was wrong!

"Saraleh, what's wrong? Is everything all right?" Steve shouted back into the phone.

"No... it's not, Steve. Yoram... your grandpa had a heart attack and he's in the hospital!"

"Is he okay?" Steve burst back.

"He's in intensive care!" Saraleh whimpered, bursting into tears, prompting her granddaughter to take the phone.

"Steve, this is your cousin Yael. Yoram had a big heart attack. It happened at work while he was inspecting one of the cottages the kibbutz is building. He took a bad fall, too, which made things even worse. He's in intensive care now, but it doesn't look good. We thought you should know."

"Yael, I'm getting the next plane out. I'll be there as soon as I can!" Steve yelled into the phone, and hung up before realizing he hadn't said goodbye. Yael would understand, he reasoned.

*   *   *

The next thing Steve thought about was to call his father. He had to know what happened!

"Hello..."

"Hello, Dad..."

"Steven... Is everything all right? You usually don't call this late."

"Dad... listen! Grandpa's had a heart attack. It doesn't sound good! Tomorrow afternoon I'm taking a direct flight out of Newark to Tel Aviv. I know you and Grandpa haven't gotten along, but I thought maybe... maybe you'd want to come with me."

"Ah... I don't know..."

"Dad, it's serious! I spoke to his wife and granddaughter. They called me."

"Well..."

"Listen, Dad, I don't have much time. I have to pack. My friends are flying me to Butte tonight and, from there, I'm catching a connecting flight into Newark. My friends have been really great. They arranged everything for me, even an emergency passport. Let me give you the flight information and you can decide, okay? Do you have a pen?"

"Wait a second... okay, go ahead!"

"Okay... it's El Al flight number LY028, leaving Newark on the sixteenth – that's tomorrow – at four PM and arriving in Tel Aviv at 09:35 the next morning."

"That's flight No. LY028?"

"Right! Dad, please listen to me. I know Grandpa would want you to come. He loves you very much. He told me so."

"I'm not sure, Steven."

"Dad, listen! If you decide to come, meet me at Newark Airport at the El Al counter as early as possible. They said they still have a couple of seats available and they give special consideration to medical emergencies."

"All right, Steven. I'm not sure if I'll be flying over with you, but in any case, I'll meet you at the airport – at the El Al counter. I'll call your mother and let her know what's happened, so don't worry, okay?"

"Okay, Dad, thanks! But, please – think about coming with me. It would make Grandpa so happy to see you."

"I'll see you tomorrow, Steven. Have a good flight into Newark."

"Thanks, Dad. See you soon… bye!"

"Goodbye, Steven."

TELEGRAM

FROM Steve Friedman Missoula International Airport Missoula, Montana U.S.A.

RECEIVED AT Friedman Family Kibbutz Misgav-Am Israel, 16 Sept. 03

ARRIVING TEL AVIV EL AL FLIGHT LY028 AT 09:35 17 SEPTEMBER STOP WILL CALL FROM AIRPORT STOP STEVE

On board El Al Flight No. LY028

El Al's non-stop flight from New York (Newark) to Tel Aviv was booked solid – at least in "Coach", where Steve was seated about half way down the right-hand side – next to a window. His father was in Business Class, also full, but with a little more leg room and a lot less noise and confusion than its less expensive counter part at the back of the plane.

Rosh Hashanah was only ten days away and many religious Jews from the New York area wanted to spend the holidays with family in Israel. We're talking moms, dads, grandparents and all the "step-ladder" children down to the baby in mom or dad's arms – usually dad's. If they could walk, they ran, up and down the narrow isles and their yelps of laughter and other such noises could even be heard clearly above the constant hum of the giant Rolls-Royce engines powering the 747 Jumbo Jet across the Atlantic.

"Thank God Dad's in Business Class," Steve thought to himself. *"This would drive him up a wall!"*

This was the first time Steve had actually come into contact with ultra-orthodox religious Jews and it was quite a curiosity for him. Growing up in a secular Jewish home and community, his only real sense of his own Jewish identity came from his brief stint of Hebrew School prior to his bar mitzvah, and the celebration of the two main Jewish holidays of Rosh Hashanah and Yom Kippur. Every year the bulk of the Jewish community would finally show up at temple, ostensibly to reconnect with their Jewish heritage, while listening to the rabbi's inspirational sermon, and to pledge their yearly dona-tion (tax deductible, of course) to the Jewish National Fund; which in recent years has been serving local Jewish charities rather than Israeli institutions. However, if the truth be told, showing up at temple twice a year was simply to see… and be seen.

And then of course, who could forget Passover; a great excuse to have a delectable holiday dinner, along with the re-telling of the Moses story and how he led the Children of Israel out of Egypt and on to the Promised Land… after a forty-year trek in the desert. All this not withstanding, Steve's recollection of the Passover holiday was mainly that fabulous dinner called a Seder, which was even bigger and more sumptuous than Thanksgiving!

But now, Steve was in the presence of these very serious minded co-religionists who seemed to take the rituals of Judaism quite strictly... and somberly. The men, dressed entirely in black, bobbed and weaved back and forth – vigorously – almost in a trance-like state as they chanted the evening prayers so intensely that Steve just stared in amazement. It was like nothing he had ever witnessed before. And when it came time for morning prayers and the laying of tefillin; the ritualistic binding of the arm – tightly – with black leather straps while *davening*, it awakened in Steve a painful reminder of the one time he also participated in that strange ritual – at his bar mitzvah six years earlier. He had long since forgotten the religious significance of that uniquely fashioned "tourniquet".

It wasn't long after morning prayers were concluded that breakfast was being served. Although it had been evident since boarding, that most – if not all – of the passengers on this non-stop flight to Tel Aviv were Jewish, this would be Steve's first real awareness that the airline itself was also Jewish. Of course he knew that El Al was Israel's national airline. The captain had even welcomed the passengers on board both in English and in Hebrew. But what was about to happen truly boggled his mind and not only brought on a sense of nostalgia, but also a strange and unexpected feeling of "belonging".

As a secular Jew, Steve observed and related to only a few of the most popular traditions associated with Jewish cultural life in America. One of those "traditions" was about to re-appear right before his eyes – and nose – 30,000 feet up in the sky. As the stewardess set down a breakfast tray, laden with his favorite Sunday morning brunch of bagels and lox – and the creamiest of cream cheeses (Philadelphia brand), he knew he was at home. No other airline in the world would serve this particular breakfast – only a Jewish airline. A bagel and lox breakfast was one of those little "Jewish things", that acted as a bastion of defense against total assimilation into the American gentile world, characterized, by *their* all-time favorite breakfast of bacon and eggs with a side order of hash browns. This surprise "Jewish" breakfast treat was only the first in a series of unique experiences in store for Steve that particular Wednesday morning on board El Al's flight No. LY028 en route to Israel's Mediterranean metropolis of Tel Aviv-Yaffo.

Some time after the breakfast trays had been cleared, an announcement came from the cockpit – this time though, only in English.

> *"Ladies and Gentlemen, good morning. This is your captain speaking. On behalf of the crew and myself, we hope you've had a pleasant flight. In about five minutes we'll be passing over the coastline of Israel. You'll be able to see Tel Aviv directly below and on this clear morning you should be able to see as far as Ashkelon in the south and Haifa Bay and beyond in the north. We'll be making our approach to Ben-Gurion Airport from the east, so we'll be banking over the Judean Hills and you'll be able to see Jerusalem quite clearly. We'll be landing in about 15 minutes, so please fasten your seat belts and again, we hope you've had a pleasant flight and thank you for flying El Al.*

As worried as Steve was about his grandfather, he couldn't help being caught up in the excitement which followed the captain's announcement. As all those moms, dads and even grandparents busily rounded up all their broods and, of course, the last minute "pit stops" for young and old alike, Steve sensed that landing in Tel Aviv would be "different" – not scary, just different than on other commercial airlines and in other cities around the world. The whole atmosphere was different. Usually during landing procedures, most passengers are quite pensive and very obedient to the instructions given to them by the pilot and crew. Not so on this flight. Simply put, it was pure chaos! Even though the "seat belt" sign was lit, practically no one was in their seat. Those "men in black" were not only standing, but they were busily taking down all sorts of packages and hand luggage from the compartments above their seats.

"What's the rush?" Steve was thinking to himself. "*There's plenty of time after we land!*" With that thought in mind, Steve just turned away in disbelief, preferring rather to enjoy the magnificent view of the Israeli coastline below.

And then came another distraction. Steve heard singing from the back of the plane. No... it wasn't religious "chanting", it was real singing. It was loud and it was infectious!

"Who's singing?", Steve asked his seating companion.

"Oh they're probably a bunch of yeshiva students spending the holidays in Israel", came the reply.

"But they're dressed differently than these other religious people", Steve replied, motioning to the men in black. "They look more like hippies, rather than religious students", Steve observed.

"You're right!" the man said with a slight chuckle. "But they are religious and they're politically very right wing!"

"What do you mean?" Steve queried next.

"They identify with the settlers in the West Bank and Gaza", came the over-simplified answer to a very complicated political divide in Israel.

"Oh...!" was Steve's only response to a political situation in Israel he knew absolutely nothing about. He went back to observing the extraordinary view the captain had mentioned a few moments before.

As the giant aircraft circled over the Judean Hills, heading for Ben-Gurion International Airport, the singing from the back of the plane continued, becoming more intense and enthusiastic as the plane neared the airport. Even though it was sung in Hebrew, Steve understood the simple words repeated over and over again. It was about peace – *Shalom*.

"*Hevenu shalom aleichem, hevenu shalom aleichem, hevenu shalom, shalom, shalom aleichem.*"
We bring peace to you, we bring peace to you, we bring peace, peace, peace to all of you!"

It was indeed "infectious" and as the plane descended toward its final approach, Steve found himself humming along. He couldn't help it! When the wheels touched down onto the runway, Steve had one more surprise in store for him on this – his maiden flight to Israel. It was another "first" and as far as he knew unique to El Al and their passengers landing in Israel. Everyone… simply everyone, including those very serious religious people began to clap with great enthusiasm.

"What's this for?" Steve asked his seating companion, also clapping away with much gusto!

"Tradition!" came the one word response. "Tradition!" he repeated. Steve joined in and enjoyed every minute of this special El Al experience.

Disembarking at Ben-Gurion International Airport

With the congestion and confusion of 350 or so passengers exiting the huge aircraft – both from the front and rear of the plane – it wasn't until the delays at passport control that father and son were finally able to hook up. Having both their passports duly stamped, they flowed with the crowds into the baggage retrieval section of the airport. There, ten or more of those oblong rotundas were spitting out luggage of all shapes and sizes onto rotating blades that just kept coming around and around, each time with a few more suitcases, bags, boxes and other nondescript items – all waiting to be picked-up by their owners. The first trick however, was to find the right rotunda. Steve finally spotted a sign scrawled in red marker reading LY028.

"That's us, Dad!", he shouted over similar shouts by fellow passengers. "I'll get a cart and you watch out for our bags… okay!"

"Okay, Steven." came the short and somewhat irritated reply. It had been a long tiring flight – even in Business Class.

After about half an hour's wait, Steve spotted their two small suitcases, snatched them adroitly from the rotating blades and led the way toward the exit. Once there, they encountered signs and lights indicating two different directions. The red light was for *"something to declare"* and the green light meant *"nothing to declare."* They took the path of least resistance and although security guards were making spot checks, they passed through the non-declaration line without incident.

"Thank God we're out of that mess!" Michael said, as they exited through automatic doors leading into a reception area filled to capacity with anxious faces. The atmosphere was festive and electric with excitement and anticipation, as relatives waited for their loved ones to emerge. But Steve's mood was anything but festive. His thoughts had returned to the reason for their long journey – his ailing grandfather.

The first thing on Steve's mind was to get some Israeli currency, find a public telephone and call the kibbutz as he had written in the telegram. But before he had had a chance to reconnoiter, something in the crowd caught his eye. It was a hand printed sign with his name on it, held up high by a pretty soldier girl.

"That must be Yael", he said to his Dad. "That's really nice of her to meet us at the airport", he continued, as he led the way through the crowd over to the girl in uniform.

"Are you Yael?", Steve asked – already knowing it was.

"Yes Steve, we got your telegram and thought we would pick you up".

"Thank you so much! Yael... this is my father. Dad this is Grandpa's Israeli granddaughter. I spoke to her on the phone".

"Hello Yael... Thank you for picking us up. How's my Dad?" Michael asked the young woman, who was obviously not quite ready to respond – at least not in the middle of the crowded reception area.

"Why don't we go over there", Yael suggested, pointing to a relatively quieter corner of the terminal. "We can talk there... if that's all right? Oh, bye the way, this is Hannan, the secretary of the kibbutz", introducing the man who had accompanied her to the airport.

With handshakes all around, the foursome made their way over to that somewhat less noisy corner – away from the crowd. Yael turned and faced father and son. This was the moment she had tried to prepare herself for... but couldn't. With tears already streaming down her cheeks she spoke the words that Steve and his father weren't ready to hear. But they were spoken all the same.

"I'm so very, very sorry to tell you this, but Yoram had another attack yesterday – in the hospital – and they weren't able to save him. He passed away late last night. We loved him very, very much!"

North by Northeast

The road leading north from the airport had changed considerably since Michael and his mother moved back to the States some 30 years before, leaving Yoram and his Zionist dreams behind. Back then – in the early '70s – Israel was slowly emerging from its first quarter-century of independence, having fought three major wars with its Arab neighbors, the last – and most traumatic – in October of '73; the Yom Kippur War... Michael remembered it well! How could he forget!

Although preoccupied with sadness at his father's passing, as well as latent feelings of remorse about the thirty-year hiatus between them, Michael couldn't help being distracted by the physical changes to the landscape he was witnessing during the drive to the kibbutz. As they approached the southern outskirts of Tel Aviv, the highway merged into a super-modern expressway known as the "Ayalon", which cuts a swath some 500 meters wide, right through the very heart of this sprawling metropolis. Framed on either side by state-of-the-art high-rise office towers, some reaching over fifty stories high, the "Ayalon" was the civil engineering solution to the enormous traffic congestion which had accompanied the country's extraordinary industrial and high-tech growth in the last thirty years.

Sitting in the passenger seat next to Hannan, Michael asked many questions of the driver, whose quiet manner and well-informed answers served as a welcome relief to the sadness of the moment. Steve and Yael sat in the back, talking softly, sharing their feelings – becoming family.

Since rush-hour traffic had long since passed, it only took 10 or so minutes for the kibbutz car to clear the Tel Aviv city limits and link up with the coastal road heading north toward the port city of Haifa. Within another quarter of an hour, they were already passing the Mediterranean resort town of Netanya, with its luxury seafront hotels clearly visible from the highway. Michael remembered Netanya of the 70s as a somewhat seedy urban area.

"What a difference a few decades make!" he thought to himself in amazement… and then it came to him. One of those hotels is where that terrorist attack took place last year on the first night of Passover. He shivered with the thought, but quickly put it out of his mind as they sped by scenes of new commercial and residential developments that read almost like a travelogue about Israel in the 21st century. As Hannan filled in the verbal commentary of what Michael was viewing out the window, time passed without notice. At the Zichron Yaacov interchange, about 20 miles south of Haifa, they began heading east; inland, across the scenic agricultural valleys which dominate this area of the country. Steve and Yael were still talking softly in back, oblivious to the change in direction.

As they traveled farther east, Michael was surprised to see picturesque Arab villages dotting the landscape, with their distinctive minarets clearly distinguishing them as Arab rather than Jewish settlements. He had forgotten that Israeli Arabs live within Israel proper and not in the so-called "territories".

"They're not the Palestinians who are sending suicide bombers to kill Israelis," he reasoned. *"But what's the difference between them?"* he questioned silently. *"They're both Arab Muslims."* He decided it was just too complicated a question to ask Hannan… and certainly not an appropriate time to discuss politics. *"No politics!"* he yelled to himself – silently.

About an hour's drive inland from the coastal highway, they reached a large cross-road known as the Golani Junction, in honor of the Golani Brigade who fought there during the War of Independence.

"Today its claim to fame is an impressive soldiers' memorial and... a McDonald's restaurant", Hannan volunteered, in a tone that obviously showed his displeasure with the latter. "But...", he added, countering his own lack of enthusiasm for the fast-food chain being located in such a pastoral and historic location, "...it's one of the few places in the country where Jews and Arabs can sit down side by side – in peace – and enjoy a "Big-Mac". Michael was impressed, but didn't comment... keeping to his self-imposed restriction on "talking politics". Hannan turned left, heading due north into a geographic area of the country known as the Lower Galilee.

As they drove through the gentle foothills of this ancient landscape... Michael remembered! How could he forget! How could he forget the journey that had changed his young life – as well as that of both his parents? That journey, so long ago, might not have been traveled on this modern, beautifully paved highway, but he did pass through the very same hills and gullies they were traveling through now... Michael remembered! How could he forget!

Thirty-three years before, their ship, the "Nili", had docked at Haifa Port early in the morning and by midday they were riding in a very large taxi, with all their baggage lashed to its roof. They were driving to a place way up in the mountains called a kibbutz... Michael remembered! How could he forget!

Back then, at the tender age of 10, his childhood had been rudely interrupted by his parents' decision to move half-way around the world to a country that didn't even speak English. He didn't even have a say in the matter. One evening they came to him before bedtime and told him about this crazy idea they had about moving to Israel. Within less than a year, he had to say goodbye to all his friends and travel by boat to a new life half-way around the world. He was terrified!... Michael remembered! How could he forget!

They had sailed out of New York Harbor on a huge Italian ocean liner named the "Michelangelo". At the port of Genoa, Italy, they switched to an Israeli merchant ship and sailed for Haifa. The whole experience was both exciting and scary at the same time – mostly scary! And now, Michael remembered it all – driving through the very same countryside, to the very same place in the mountains. But this time, it was to bury his father. Tears came to his eyes, but he turned toward the window and wiped them away before Hannan could notice... Michael remembered everything! How could he forget!

The conversation in the back of the car could only be described as intense and emotional. Both Yael and Steve had been very close to Yoram and their individual bond with their grandfather had now become their bond. Sharing feelings seemed as natural to them as if they had known each other all their lives. They felt more like brother and sister rather than distant cousins who had just met for the first time.

As the journey north zigzagged its way through the extraordinary beauty of the Galilee, Steve couldn't help but notice. After all, he was a nature lover and the Galilee is surely one of Mother Nature's dearest of projects. It's certainly not as grandiose as the Rockies – for sure – or even as rugged as the Appalachians of eastern North America, but it's as beautifully sculptured and contoured as any of Mother Nature's more "gentle works" scattered around the globe. Both Yael's presence and the beauty... and authenticity of this biblical backdrop, seemed to form a cocoon around Steve, easing the pain and calming the emotions of a great loss. It was so hard for him to imagine not being able to sit down and write to his very special pen pal. He had lost his best friend – and confidant.

Gradually, the journey northward had also risen several hundred meters above sea level, as it made its way through the Galilean countryside. Around every twist and turn in the road, lay a unique view; pleasant to the eye... and calming to the soul. At one point, however, high above the picturesque Kinneret, the bird's-eye view of this celebrated lake and its environs was nothing short of spectacular! A small kiosk off the main road served as a handy excuse for a welcome "pit-stop" and coffee break. As the foursome gazed out in silence at the extraordinary panorama below, only the sounds of nature could be heard. Words of any kind would have been inappropriate.

Continuing on, they were now entering what is referred to as the Upper Galilee, defined geographically by its central agricultural valley called the Hula; once a vast mosquito infested swampland, and which now cradles many kibbutzim (farming communities) in its drained fertile acreage. On the western edge of the valley, a low mountain range reaches northward toward the Lebanese border. On the eastern edge, a high plateau known as the Golan Heights makes its way from the south, rising dramatically – directly opposite Kibbutz Misgav-Am – into the magnificent multi-peaked summits of Mt. Hermon, over 2000 meters above sea level. Other than his beloved Saraleh, this mountain was Yoram's greatest love. He awoke every morning to the sunrise peeking over its distinctive silhouette in the pre-dawn sky, and he ended each day delighting in the array of colorful hues thrown onto its luminous surface by the diffused rays of light at sundown. To the people who knew him best, the mountain simply became "Yoram's mountain"... an honor he accepted with great delight.

The road north to the kibbutz now paralleled the central valley and the heights beyond. At one point along the way, close to one of the first farming villages in the area named Rosh Pinna, Mt. Hermon came into sight on the north-eastern horizon. Although a bit obscured by the slight haze of a typical September day, Steve could now see for himself what his grandfather had always talked about in his letters. It was a beautiful mountain – for sure! Although stoic till this point in time, tears came to his eyes which he could not hide from his new soul mate, Yael. She understood without a word spoken.

The final noteworthy landmark on their journey to Yoram and Saraleh's home was the frontier town of Kiryat Shmona, less than 10 kilometers from the Lebanese border. Although it took only about five to seven minutes to travel from one side of town to the other, Steve noticed two large shopping malls and a bustling populace, even though the town had endured endless Katyusha rocket attacks in the late 90s, from the Hizbullah terrorists across the border.

"Pretty hearty people!" he thought to himself as he watched young and old alike going about their lives as if they were in the center of "middle America", rather than living so close to a hostile border. As they passed through town, Yael mentioned that they'd be turning off the main road in a few minutes and onto the mountain road leading to the kibbutz.

"It's only about a kilometer outside of town", she added, knowing that it had been a long tiring trip for both Steve and his Dad. Their journey to say goodbye to father and grandfather would soon be over. Within a minute or so a road sign indicated a left-hand turn toward two kibbutzim. The first was Kfar Giladi, only a few hundred meters up the road. The second was Kibbutz Misgav-Am – 10 kilometers further up the mountain.

Passing the entrance to the lower kibbutz, Yael pointed to the very top of a high ridge ahead of them saying rather informatively…

"That's the kibbutz way up there!" Although Steve was really quite impressed, he said nothing. His emotions were too close to the surface and he had to stay in control. Michael also remained silent, as the memories of this mountain road flooded back into his consciousness; although as he recalled – back then – it was more like a dirt and gravel path meandering its way up the mountain, as compared to this newly paved asphalt surface.

As the road twisted and turned up the mountain like a "giant slalom" in reverse, the view of the valley far below was really impressive, but Steve and his father remained silent. After about 10–12 minutes of traveling up the mountain, the road leveled off revealing an extraordinary panorama of the valley and its guardian – Mt. Hermon. Steve's simple, yet obvious observation said it all…

"It's really very beautiful up here!" Yael nodded. At the entrance to the kibbutz, a large steel gate slid back, allowing the car to pass. Hannan waved to the soldier on duty, saying with a distinct sense of pride in his voice…

"The Golani Brigade guards our kibbutz!"

Three Days in the Galilee

Author's Note: *During the 1970s Kibbutz Misgav-Am built innovative terraced housing units which followed the 30° slope of their mountain-top village. Back then, it was considered to be quite unique for its time, and is still today the envy of many a city dweller.*

Yoram and Saraleh's home was on a middle level adjacent to the central parking area. It only took a minute or two for the foursome to arrive at an open door where many of the kibbutz members had come to share in Saraleh's private grieving as well as their own loss of a dear friend and devoted member of this special mountain community.

Realizing who the newcomers were, most of the friends and neighbors began leaving in order to give privacy to Saraleh and her family, who were now meeting their American relatives for the very first time – and under the saddest of circumstances. It had always been Yoram's fondest hope that he and his son would someday make peace with one another. Saraleh had shared Yoram's dream for as many years as they were together – but it was not to be. It had also been Steve's fondest hope that his dad and grandfather would forgive each other for the past. It just didn't happen… and now it was too late.

Hannan hugged Saraleh and left, leaving her in the loving embrace of her intimate little family – daughter Tami, son-in-law Avi and her two wonderful granddaughters Yael and Ronit. But now, there were two more people who were to become part of this intimacy. Two people she had wanted to meet in person for many, many years – but not like this! And she began to cry. There was no need to hold back. These newcomers were Yoram's flesh and blood. In a hesitant and emotional English, she began to express what Yoram had always wanted to say to his son… but never got the chance.

"Michael, your father loved you very, very much and he missed you for such a long time. I'm so sorry he never got a chance to tell you that in person". With those clear, unembellished words, Saraleh broke the silence of a thirty-year barrier between father and son. Unexpectedly, Michael was moved to the point of tears and incredulously found himself comforted by the woman who had not only "replaced" his mother, but had given his father the happiness and contentment that sadly, she never could. Both cried unashamedly, finally tearing down that wall of silence which had caused so much pain and heartache for both men – for so long. For the rest of that day, and into the early evening hours, the new extended family began to talk; solidifying their familial ties; becoming one unified family, rather than just the temporary inclusion of its American branch.

By now, the hour was really getting late and Michael and Steve were both showing signs of their physical and emotional exhaustion from the events of the last forty-eight hours. The funeral would begin in the late afternoon of the next day. Now it was time to sleep. Yael led Steve and his father to a guest house where everything had been prepared for their stay – for as long as they wanted.

Both men slept till noon and beyond. Avi was delegated to wake them up with some strong coffee. It did the trick! But it was already after two o'clock before Steve and Michael made their way over to Saraleh's. Just the family was there. Everyone else would be meeting at the communal dining hall at four o'clock to begin the walk to the kibbutz cemetery. There was still time for the family to be together for just a little while longer before that final journey to say goodbye. Friends had brought over everything from cakes and cookies to casseroles. No one was really hungry, but they ate anyway. It was just something to do while they waited.

It was a little after 3:30 when the seven mourning souls emerged from Saraleh and Yoram's home and made their way across the parking lot to the entrance to the dining hall. A few close friends had arrived early and shared a moment with Saraleh and the family before they disappeared into a small meeting-room where Yoram lay in a plain pine box, honor-guarded by two of his closest friends. With these last few moments of privacy before the procession, the family allowed themselves to cry without inhibition. Afterwards, they would do their best to be stoic and dignified. Yoram would have appreciated that.

Outside, hundreds had gathered; not only members of the kibbutz, but old friends from many parts of the country who had known Saraleh and Yoram throughout the years, had now come to pay their last respects. When a tractor and flatbed trailer pulled up outside, one of Yoram's friends motioned to the family that it was time to go. As they emerged into the crowd outside, two other pallbearers entered and within moments, the four men brought the casket outside and set it down gently onto the flatbed. And the tractor began to move – ever so slowly – setting the pace for the procession which followed. Buckets of freshly picked flowers had been placed nearby, so that everyone might choose a small bouquet to leave as a symbol of their presence at this final ceremony of respect for a man that many loved and all admired. He would be greatly missed.

After almost a quarter of an hour of meandering its way through the narrow passages separating the terraces, the procession came to the edge of a beautiful pine forest – and entered by way of a dirt path no wider than the width of the tractor itself. The tall trees and the late afternoon hour allowed the sunlight to enter only at a low oblique angle, causing the rays of light to appear as if they were darting in and out, as each wave of mourners passed by. It was quite beautiful – hauntingly so. It was almost like an anesthetic; dulling the pain – at least temporarily. But Mother Nature's medication was about to wear off abruptly when the forest opened up onto a small rocky plateau overlooking the valley. There, on two natural terraces, stood the grey and white headstones of loved ones from the past, lined up like soldiers at attention – guarding this sacred site. Now, Yoram was about to join their sentry.

Just to the right of one of the headstones was a freshly dug grave with two wooden planks and heavy-duty ropes spanning the void. Two brawny men stood on either side as four others lifted the casket off the flatbed and brought it to rest on the planks. A microphone and speakers had been set up close by. Now, all of Yoram and Saraleh's friends gathered around in a large semi-circle surrounding the family and Yoram's final resting place – directly across the valley from his beloved mountain.

Needless to say, Yoram would have been embarrassed by all the wonderful things said about him that afternoon, but he would also have been humbled and touched by the loving words spoken by his friends as they said their final goodbyes. Some even spoke partly in English, in order to allow Yoram's son and grandson to really understand how they felt about their friend and fellow kibbutz member. Steve wasn't surprised by the outpouring of love and affection expressed that afternoon. He knew his grandfather was a very special person. Yet hearing those loving words from strangers was a special gift which he could now take back with him as part of his own private memories of his pen pal, best friend… and soul mate. Michael, on the other hand, really didn't know his father and the words spoken didn't seem to fit the picture of the man he had despised for so many years. But for now, he'd have to put all that confusion aside. He had a duty to perform. Avi had given him a black yarmulke and an English transliteration of the mourners Kaddish. This was his responsibility – and no one else's.

"Yitgadal v'yitkadash shmay rabba. B'al'ma divra chir'ootay v'yamlich mal'chutay, b'chayaychon uvyomaychon uv'chayei d'chol beit yisra-el, ba-agala uviz'man kariv v'imru Amein.
Y'hei shmay rabba m'vorach l'alam ul'amay al'maya... Oseh

shalom bimromav, hu ya-aseh shalom aleinu v'al kol yisra-el v'im'ru Amein."

After stumbling over the difficult pronunciations, Michael finally finished the prayer, visibly shaken by the experience, as well as the intense emotions surrounding him. He had never imagined himself doing what he had just done... or where he'd be at this very moment. As the crowd began to disperse, only Steve's voice brought him back into focus.

"Look Dad... That's Grandpa's mountain! Look at those colors... It's really beautiful, isn't it?"

"Yes it is, Steven", Michael replied softly – almost reverently.

The walk back was solemn. No one chatted. Michael and Steve stayed at Saraleh's till almost midnight – until fatigue simply took over. As father and son walked back to the guest house, neither spoke. It had been an incredible day. The swiftness and finality of events were beyond their immediate comprehension. Their own personal dialogue would have to wait for another time, another place. Now they just wanted to sleep.

The next day – Friday – was going to be a most difficult day for the family. It was the day when the kibbutz members would be coming to pay a *shiva* call; starting at about ten o'clock in the morning and lasting until sundown at the beginning of the Sabbath. It was also going to be Steve and Michael's last day on the kibbutz. They'd decided to spend a few days in Jerusalem before their flight home on Tuesday evening. It seemed that both father and son had a need to touch base with their roots, and what better place to do so than in Israel's capital city and an emotional pilgrimage to touch the ancient stones of the Western Wall – Judaism's most sacred site.

An unspoken yet understood obligation of everyone in the immediate family, except for Saraleh of course, was to greet everyone and to try and make small talk in order to help deflect the sadness of the moment. Since everyone spoke a simple, yet understandable English, It wasn't that difficult for Michael and Steve to initiate conversations with the strangers, some of whom they recognized from the funeral the day before. Tami and the girls served everyone from the lovely food platters brought over by loving friends and neighbors.

It was about three o'clock when Michael decided to leave for a little while and walk over to the cemetery – alone. It was time to have a private talk with his father. It had been over thirty years and he had so much to say to the man he never got to know. Maybe it wasn't too late after all.

MICHAEL'S SOLILOQUY

"Hi Dad... It's been a long time... I want to say something to you, but I don't know exactly how to start. So please be patient with me... okay? I was only about fourteen when Mom and I left Israel, so I'm trying to remember what happened to us back then and what caused us so much pain – for so long! Of course it was that awful war and living in those shelters for so long. But it wasn't so bad for me. I had all my friends. It was even kind of... kind of adventurous living underground for a while. But for Mom... it was different. Israel was at war... and this kibbutz was only a few kilometers from the front line. It was so close we could smell the war, Dad. It was that close! And Mom had all that responsibility for the children. She couldn't show them – or anyone else – how frightened she was. Only years later, she told me how hard she tried not to show it – especially to you.

And you, Dad... you were such a gung-ho Israeli. She tried to talk to you, but you were always out with your new buddies, trying to be more Israeli than the Israelis. It really hurt her. She really didn't have anybody to talk to back then. She was miserable, Dad... and she kept it all inside until the war was finally over, and we could come up from those... those catacombs. Dad... Don't you understand! She only moved to Israel because of you. Because somewhere along the way you became a Zionist. She only came along for the ride because she loved you... very very much. And probably still does. I called her last night, Dad – after the funeral. She cried, Dad... She cried. She never remarried. It was always you. Never anyone else. Can you imagine how devastated she was when you refused to come back to the States, and she realized then that you loved Israel more than you loved her? Can you imagine how she felt, Dad? She felt betrayed! You loved a country and an idea more than you loved her! She never forgave you for that... and neither did I.

But you know what, Dad, that was thirty years ago... and thirty years is a long time to carry around all that... that bitterness. It's enough already! You and I both missed out on each other – and that's a damn shame! I never got to know this extraordinary guy who everybody seems to love and admire – and who just happens to be my father. And you, Dad, you missed out on seeing your only son growing into manhood. And I'm sorry for both our losses... You know what, Dad, you never got to meet my first girlfriend... you never got to give me the keys to the car for the very first time – after I got my license. And you never got to see me off to the senior prom, all decked out in that white jacket and tie... and that silly maroon cummerbund. I really did look pretty cool. I'm sorry Mom never sent you a picture. You weren't there for my college graduation either. I never even had the chance to tell you I graduated cum laude. But the most important milestone in my life that you missed, Dad, was the birth of my son – your grandson... and that was the biggest shame of all.

But then something absolutely amazing happened. Fate seems to have taken a hand in all this "missing-out" business, in order to correct a major injustice to an innocent – my son Steven. A grandson should know his grandfather. And so the events unfolded. It all started because we were a bit over-protective of Steven, when he wanted to go on this hike with his Scout troop in the middle of winter. Whatever possessed him to write to you I'll never know, but that first letter triggered a bonding between the two of you that was a source of great envy on my part... Steven and I have never been that close and I'm admitting to you now that I was even a little jealous. Isn't that childish... but it's true. But at the same time, Dad, I was really grateful when you and Steven got to know each other through your letters. I almost screwed it up for a while when I stopped you from writing. But again... after a while, fate took over and the two of you became more than just pen-pals. You became friends. I wish you and I had been friends, Dad... maybe not really friends. I just needed my father and I had to grow up without you. I never got to know you, Dad, like these people here on the kibbutz. They know you and they all seem to love you. I guess you're a pretty special guy... and you're my Dad. At least I got to hear all those great things they said about you yesterday. Maybe Steven can help me get to know you. He's a great kid and I love him very much. Anyway, Dad, I just wanted to have this little talk with you before we go home. It makes me happy that you're surrounded by all the people you love and who love you. And… you're even within sight of your beloved mountain. She really is beautiful. Rest in peace, Dad… Shalom."

*   *   *

Epilogue

Dear Yael,

Sorry it's taken me so long to write to you after returning home.
I spent about a week in New Jersey with both Mom and Dad before
flying back out here to Montana. It feels really good to be in the
mountain country again. My friends here have been really great.
They know how close I was to Grandpa and they all shared in my
loss. I'm pretty lucky to have such good friends – especially Dale.
I told you about him. He and his wife Sally Jo and their daughter
Tammy are my family out here in Montana. I even help Tammy
with her homework sometimes. She's ten... and really bright!

Anyway, before I left New Jersey, I had a long talk with Dad
about Grandpa and I think he's come to some kind of peace about
the past. His bitterness about events that took place so long ago
was a heavy burden to carry around all those years... and now he's
free! He actually cried in front of me, which was an incredible step
of sharing for Dad. Before our trip to Israel and Grandpa's passing,
he would never have allowed himself to break down like that – in
my presence. We were never that close, but that's changing – slowly.
I think the special relationship I had with Grandpa seems to be
the catalyst that's bringing Dad and me closer together. I'm really
happy for him. Now maybe he can move on and remember his father in a different light. I hope so! I'm only sorry Grandpa's dream

of reconciliation with his son didn't happen during his lifetime... Maybe he knows after all.

I called Dad last night and he reminded me that today is Yom Kippur. I don't think he's going to temple, but it is a day of reflection – for all of us. Yael, I have to tell you honestly that I still find myself in utter disbelief that Grandpa is no longer with us. It all happened so quickly. First came your phone call, then the flight to Israel... and then the news. I can still picture you at the airport, tears streaming down your cheeks as you told us the news. Maybe it was the effects of the long plane flight, but your words and all the events of that first day just didn't seem real. It wasn't until the next day, as we were walking to the cemetery, that I began to realize I would no longer be able to share my life with this extraordinary person who had played such an important role in my life and who in turn shared his life, his wisdom and his memories with me. We truly were the best of friends and I miss him very, very much.

As I think back over the years, it does seem truly amazing how our 'pen pal' relationship developed into such a strong bond of friendship between us. Even though there was a half-century gap in our ages and life experiences, we seem to have been cut from the same mould. We were, in a sense, contemporaries of the soul. And that was our bond. More than any other person in my life, Grandpa gave me counsel – and the courage – to make independent decisions that will affect the rest of my life. He was in every sense of the word my mentor, as I emerged from the blissful years of high school into the uncertainties of the future – especially now that my parents are separated and no longer provide the stability of "home base" that I had while I was growing up.

Grandpa also gave me a very special gift. In his letters, he challenged me to think about things I would ordinarily not have thought about – at least at this stage in my life. In that context, he opened up a window of awareness about my heritage that broadened my Jewish identity; much more so than those few years of Hebrew school prior to my bar mitzvah and going to temple once a year on the High Holidays. I once asked him why he had to move to Israel to be (or feel) more Jewish. I think I understand now. Being a Jew in the Diaspora is one thing, but being a Jew who has made a commitment to live and help rebuild the ancient land of our fathers is quite a different kind of Jew. And that's who Grandpa was – a proud Jew, a committed Zionist and an Israeli patriot. He felt an almost boastful pride in being a part of the modern renaissance of the Jewish People who were returning to their biblical homeland. It was all happening during his lifetime and there was no way in the world he was going to miss the journey.

Yael, at this point in time I have no idea what my future will bring vis-à-vis my connection to Israel. But I do know that Grandpa helped me to see – and feel – my Jewish identity in a much broader scope than my limited Jewish education here in the States. Maybe someday I'll come to the same conclusions that he did and make aliyah – or maybe not. Right now, I'm at the very beginning of my own journey. First on the agenda is getting my degree in forestry (after a year's stint as a ranch hand, that is). Actually I'm really looking forward to the experience. I'll write you all about it. In the meantime, please keep in touch. You're my Israeli connection now. I promise you'll see me again. Who knows, the Jewish National Fund maintains a lot of forest lands in Israel. Maybe someday they'll need a guy like me. Please give my love to the whole family and especially to Saraleh. Take care of yourself soldier girl – and be safe!

Love,

Steve.

HOLOCAUST MEMORIAL CENTER
28123 Orchard Lake Road
Farmington Hills, MI 48334-3738